LANGUAGE AND LITERACY SERIES

Dorothy S. Strickland and Celia Genishi, SERIES EDITORS

Young Adult Literature and the New Literary Theories: Developing Critical Readers in Middle School
ANNA O. SOTER

Literacy Matters: Writing and Reading the Social Self
ROBERT P. YAGELSKI

Building Family Literacy in an Urban Community
RUTH D. HANDEL

Children's Inquiry: Using Language to Make Sense of the World
JUDITH WELLS LINDFORS

Engaged Reading: Processes, Practices, and Policy Implications
JOHN T. GUTHRIE and DONNA E. ALVERMANN, Editors

Learning to Read: Beyond Phonics and Whole Language
G. BRIAN THOMPSON and TOM NICHOLSON, Editors

So Much to Say: Adolescents, Bilingualism, and ESL in the Secondary School
CHRISTIAN J. FALTIS and PAULA WOLFE, Editors

Close to Home: Oral and Literate Practices in a Transnational Mexicano Community
JUAN C. GUERRA

Authorizing Readers: Resistance and Respect in the Teaching of Literature
PETER J. RABINOWITZ and MICHAEL W. SMITH

On the Brink: Negotiating Literature and Life with Adolescents
SUSAN HYNDS

Life at the Margins: Literacy, Language, and Technology in Everyday Life
JULIET MERRIFIELD, MARY BETH BINGMAN, DAVID HEMPHILL, and KATHLEEN P. BENNETT DeMARRAIS

One Child, Many Worlds: Early Learning in Multicultural Communities
EVE GREGORY, Editor

Literacy for Life: Adult Learners, New Practices
HANNA ARLENE FINGERET and CASSANDRA DRENNON

Children's Literature and the Politics of Equality
PAT PINSENT

The Book Club Connection: Literacy Learning and Classroom Talk
SUSAN I. MCMAHON and TAFFY E. RAPHAEL, Editors, with VIRGINIA J. GOATLEY and LAURA S. PARDO

Until We Are Strong Together: Women Writers in the Tenderloin
CAROLINE E. HELLER

Restructuring Schools for Linguistic Diversity: Linking Decision Making to Effective Programs
OFELIA B. MIRAMONTES, ADEL NADEAU, and NANCY L. COMMINS

Writing Superheroes: Contemporary Childhood, Popular Culture, and Classroom Literacy
ANNE HAAS DYSON

Opening Dialogue: Understanding the Dynamics of Language and Learning in the English Classroom
MARTIN NYSTRAND with ADAM GAMORAN, ROBERT KACHUR, and CATHERINE PRENDERGAST

Reading Across Cultures: Teaching Literature in a Diverse Society
THERESA ROGERS and ANNA O. SOTER, Editors

"You Gotta Be the Book": Teaching Engaged and Reflective Reading with Adolescents
JEFFREY D. WILHELM

Just Girls: Hidden Literacies and Life in Junior High
MARGARET J. FINDERS

The First R: Every Child's Right to Read
MICHAEL F. GRAVES, PAUL van den BROEK, and BARBARA M. TAYLOR, Editors

(Continued)

Young Adult Literature and the New Literary Theories

Developing Critical Readers in Middle School

Anna O. Soter

FOREWORD BY JAMES PHELAN

Teachers College, Columbia University
New York and London

Published by Teachers College Press, 1234 Amsterdam Avenue, New York, NY 10027

Library of Congress Cataloging-in-Publication Data

Soter, Anna O., 1946–
    Young adult literature and the new literary theories :
developing critical readers in middle school / Anna O. Soter ;
foreword by James Phelan.
      p. cm. — (Language and literacy series)
    Includes bibliographical references (p.) and index.
    ISBN 0-8077-3881-6 (cloth)
    ISBN 0-8077-3880-8 (paper)
    1. Reading (Middle school) 2. Young adult literature—Study and
teaching (Middle school) I. Title. II. Series: Language and
literacy series (New York, N.Y.)
    LB1632 .S68 1999
    428.4'071'2—dc21   99-32723

ISBN 0-8077-3880-8 (paper)
ISBN 0-8077-3881-6 (cloth)

Printed on acid-free paper

Manufactured in the United States of America

06   05   04   03   02   01   8 7 6 5 4 3 2

To Terry

Contents

Literary Theory and YAL:
Strange Bedfellows or
a Match Made in Heaven?

On first picking up *YAL and the New Literary Theories*, the prospective reader is likely to have at least three questions: What do contemporary literary theories have to do with young adult literature (YAL)? Aren't those theories developed by people who condescend to YAL, if they notice it at all? Aren't those theories designed for canonical literature written according to what we might call an aesthetic of difficulty rather than for YAL, which is written for what we might call an aesthetic of accessibility? The glory of *YAL and the New Literary Theories* is that Anna Soter answers these very good questions in surprising yet convincing ways. To the first, she says "Everything!" To the second, "Maybe, but so what?" And to the third, "Not really." These answers indicate that Soter, like all good educators, wants to change the world, beginning with changing people's perceptions and assumptions. I want to say just a few things about the logic of her effort to change assumptions about the relation between literary theory and YAL.

In saying that literary theory has everything to do with YAL, Soter is not holding out theory as a magic key to YAL or YAL as a body of sacred texts that must be treated with theoretical reverence. Instead, she starts the whole enterprise by identifying her purpose in teaching any literature: to help students become lifelong readers. Students will develop the reading habit, she reasons, if their encounters with literature are enjoyable and productive and if they learn how to do rewarding things with texts on their own. Age-appropriate, well-crafted literature will generally make its own case: Many students can feel the power of *The Island*, *Homecoming*, or *My Brother Sam Is Dead* as they read. But helping students move from the power of the reading experience to an analysis that opens up rather than closes down the text is not always so easy. Soter believes that literary theory, if used appropriately, can be a productive aid.

For Soter, theory is not a machine for grinding out interpretations but a way of generating fruitful questions about texts. Furthermore, she maintains that, by becoming aware of theories and what they can and cannot do, teachers and students can recognize that there are multiple *kinds* of questions about texts: some that focus on the reader, some on the author, others on the formal properties of texts, and still others on texts' connections to other texts and to the extratextual world. Soter is careful to point out that all these variables—author, reader, text, world—will be an inevitable part of any thoughtful analysis, and so we should think of the different questions not as setting up either/or relations among these variables (e.g., either author or reader; either text or world) but as establishing different relations among them (e.g., on this day for this text, author and world get more attention than textual features and reader).

Once we learn the details of different ways of generating questions (that is to say, the details of different theories), how do we choose which set of questions to generate for any given text? Is it an arbitrary choice? Again, we can find answers in Soter's concern with purpose. Before deciding which sets of questions to ask, we need to decide what we want to know about the text. Do we want to know how the author transformed his or her own life experience into skillful fiction? Or how the students felt while reading—and the sources of those feelings both in the text and in their experiences? Or how the text participates in a larger cultural concern with a particular issue? Or how the linguistic patterns and narrative techniques affect our interpretations? Once we make some decisions about the purpose of our analysis, we can select our questions. And, of course, there's no need to settle on a single purpose for all texts and all occasions. What we want to know about *The Island* this year may not be the same thing we will want to know about it in 5 years. Furthermore, what we may be most interested in about *The Island* can be very different from what we're most interested in about *Somewhere in the Darkness*.

But what about the text? Does it have a way to signal which sets of questions it finds most hospitable, and if so, should we start with those signals? Soter does not ask these questions directly, but it is possible to infer her answer once we consider the range of possible answers and her actual practice. Some theorists would say that the text is both mute and indifferent to interpretive theories, others that some texts respond better to some sets of questions, and still others that although a given text might seem to invite a certain set of questions, we can choose whether to accept or decline the invitation. Soter's practice suggests that she is an advocate of the third school. This advocacy is part and parcel of Soter's interest in the practical consequences of theory, and especially of her goal of creating lifelong readers. One can almost hear her voice in the classroom: "Of course we should start with the text's invitations, because they can lead us to riches. But we shouldn't stop there. It can be just as exciting to try to answer questions the text does not invite us to ask."

Having seen why Soter asserts that theory and YAL have everything to do with one other, we can more easily comprehend her answers to the other two questions her prospective reader is likely to have. In suggesting that it doesn't matter if the fashioners of theory look down on or ignore YAL, Soter, in effect, opts for a reader-oriented rather than an author-oriented stance toward theory. The attitudes of the high muckety-mucks of theory don't signify as long as we readers find the theories themselves efficacious for our encounters with YAL. Similarly, although most contemporary theories have been designed for literary works whose difficulty is part of their appeal, their usefulness need not be limited to such works. Indeed, one of the consequences of linking literary theory and YAL, as Soter does here, is to reveal even more about the sophistication of much YAL. Sophistication is not the same as difficulty (although the two may sometimes overlap). Difficulty is a measure of a text's accessibility, while sophistication is a measure of its skill in bending means to ends. Subjecting the text to the questions provided by literary theory is an excellent way of testing its sophistication. As Soter's discussions of the individual works suggest, much YAL passes the test summa cum laude.

Because Soter's own book both points to and fulfills the potential of literary theory and YAL to be mutually illuminating, it passes my test for a successful contribution to pedagogical theory and practice. My message to all prospective readers is to stop reading me and start reading Soter.

James Phelan

Acknowledgments

A book is never a single individual's accomplishment. In the process of its creation, many play an essential role in bringing it to completion. I am deeply indebted and grateful for the wonderful generosity of heart, mind, and labor that my students, family, friends, and colleagues have shown as this book moved from its inception to its publication. Perhaps most immediately connected to it in a vital way is the work of Mary Armentrout, who labored through the retyping of several drafts and their sometimes tortuous signals of "cut" here or "add" there. Knowing that she would somehow make sense of the arrows, circles, and slash marks meant I could focus on reworking the ideas and their expression. Also closely connected to the ultimate publication of this book are my wonderfully supportive and patient husband, Daniel, and son, Benjamin. I'm sure they were wondering whether it would indeed ever be finished and whether my promises of a return to a normal family life were ever going to eventuate. For their faith and tolerance and humorous putting up with the constant refrain "when I finish this book," I am also indebted to Theresa Rogers, Suzy Zimmerman, and other friends and extended family.

Without the students who generously contributed examples of their work and with whom I discussed issues about literary theory and its application in schools, this book could not have been born. Grounded as many of them were in upper elementary, middle, and secondary schools, they were a constant reminder of the purpose for this book: to bring fresh approaches to literature instruction so that their own students would become lifelong readers of literature. Some also used the questions and activities in their middle school classrooms and generously shared their stories of success or failure with them. I learned much from them. For their special contributions to this book, I would like to sincerely thank Kayoko Akiyoshi, Junko Otoshi, and Amy Kepple Strawser for their invaluable contributions to Chapter 7. In helping me strengthen my arguments on linking young adult literature and literary theory, special thanks go to Alan Bates, Charles Brown, Randy Donelson, Jennifer Edwards, Chris Imhoff, Beth Murray, Pat Schutjer, and Quinn White. For their insightful comments on various young adult novels, I wish to especially thank Travis Barrett, Andrea Ankerman, Cheryl Bebout, Donald Beck,

Alicia Kleinfelter, Sean Leary, Judy Sein, Jill McNall, Elaine Snow, and Kathleen Brooks.

While he did not know it when he graciously allowed me to sit in on one of his courses on literary theory 4 years ago, Professor James Phelan of the English Department, The Ohio State University, was the catalyst for my return to a lifelong interest: playing with the language of literature. I had felt a need to update my knowledge of literary theory, having taken the last courses in 1982 while completing a master's degree in English literature and language. The reading that participating in his class generated was the foundation for my own fresh perspectives on how we might read young adult literature and what we could then do with it in the school setting. Additionally, although incredibly busy with his teaching, writing, and administrative responsibilities, Jim also read and gave valuable feedback about the book in its later drafts; and as if I do not owe him enough, he very kindly accepted the invitation to write a foreword to it. He has been a wonderful colleague without whom this book would not have been possible.

Heartfelt thanks, too, to Mark Letcher, a Ph.D. candidate at The Ohio State University who also provided insightful and helpful feedback on more recent drafts. Mark's background as an English teacher and his extensive knowledge of literary theory kept me on track both in terms of how the book will be read by language arts and English teachers in the middle and secondary school setting as well as by those who know literary theory well.

Although I consistently misspelled her name in early drafts, Professor Deanne Bogdan, University of Toronto, has remained incredibly supportive and provided extremely helpful feedback on Chapter 8, in which I discussed my application of her response categories as she describes them her book—a book that I believe every literature teacher, whether in school or college settings, should read: *Re-Educating the Imagination: Toward a Poetics, Politics, and Pedagogy of Literary Engagement*. The thought-provoking analysis and subsequent critique of response categories that she used in the first part of this book caused me to reexamine my own assumptions about the nature of literary engagement, leading to the painful conclusion that although I thought I had left my own new critical orientation behind, it is not entirely without influence.

The heart of writing is, according to many, in the revision process. In retrospect, the first draft of this book flowed forth in a manner akin to the birthing process. But, like that birthing process, you never know quite what you're going to get and, as we all know, the birth is only the beginning of a long process of maturation during which we often need help from others. I am enormously appreciative of the reviewers' suggestions for revision—they have indeed made this a better book and I hope it lives up to what they perceived as its promise. I thank them, too, for having faith that the rough copy they received would live up to their expectations. Similarly, I don't believe thanks is an adequate expression for the thorough and thoughtful reading of the subsequently revised manuscript by the Teachers College Press development editor, Cathy McClure, and Lori Tate, the production editor. I know it was a monumental task, for I tend to focus on the vision and not notice the detail. I hope this final version does justice to her efforts. I am also indebted to Carol Chambers Collins, Acquisitions Editor of Teachers College Press for her faith, patience, and encouragement throughout the lengthy process involved in bringing this book to final form. Where and how to prod, encourage, and set firm deadlines is a delicate art and I am grateful for the consistency with which she matched her vision to mine. Finally, I am very grateful to Professors Ken Donelson (Arizona State University at Tempe), Pat Zumhagen, Linworth Alternative High, Worthington, Ohio) and Janet Hickman (The Ohio State University, Columbus) for their willingness to read and support the book.

Young Adult Literature
and the
New Literary Theories

Developing Critical Readers in Middle School

CHAPTER 1

The New Literary Theories and
Young Adult Literature: An Overview

The novelist is neither historian nor prophet: he is an explorer of existence.
(Kundera, 1988, p. 44)

*What I'm telling you is self-analysis which really is not as valuable as a person
with a more objective viewpoint, the critic, the reader who follows my works, who
can look at them and see the themes which are repeated over and over again and
that in a sense tell what the author's true vision of the world is. So what I think of
the world really is reflected through my books.*
(Zindel, quoted in Garrett & McCue, 1989, Vol. 2, pp. 257–258)

I began my career as an Australian English teacher with a passion that
began in my own high secondary school years for literary classics in all
genres of the Anglo-European tradition. Austen, Hardy, the Brontës,
George Eliot, Joyce, Waugh, and Camus; Shakespeare, Sheridan, Congreve,
Brecht, and Beckett; Browning, Pope, Chaucer, Coleridge, and T.S. Eliot
were the source of inspiration and awe. Others were added to the list during
my college years as an English major. Never once did I question the validity of their texts, the quality of their writing, or the perception of reality
offered. During the 1970s our secondary English curriculum was modi-
fied to include some young adult fiction for students who were struggling
with the adult classics my own generation had loved (some) or endured
(many). I had some disdain toward those young adult novels, selected as
they had been for the "slow" readers. Their plots seemed very thin; their
characters, superficial and too "real" to be fascinating; their themes, too
connected with contemporary teen life struggles to move the reader to
great depths and heights. Regardless, many students who had become
disenfranchised members of English classrooms loved those books, read
them voraciously, and *became* readers. But we never used them to teach
students *about* literature.

Many years and paths later, I found myself designing a graduate course
in a college of education that focused on connecting literary theories that

have emerged over the past 40 years with a selection of young adult novels that I believe can bear critical scrutiny. I typically introduce that course with a collection of excerpts from a range of classical and young adult novels. I delete author and title for each of these excerpts and ask participants to identify which excerpts they think are from "classic" adult works and which are from young adult novels. To avoid the wild guess, I ask them to be able to provide a rationale for their choices. Invariably, classics are identified as young adult literature (YAL) and vice versa. Participants are astonished at the quality of the writing in the young adult texts. We then move into discussions about how we can "save" these young adult novels from being taught in the same way many of the classics are still being taught in many secondary classrooms, because to do so would not do justice to these texts or to the students who could become engaged with the literary experience if allowed to do so.

By focusing only on young adult novels in this book, I am *not* recommending the elimination of adult classics from secondary school curricula. However, I do want to show that among young adult novels are selections that teachers can use to develop students' critical appreciation of literature. Additionally, these novels contain content that is more directly relevant to teenagers and their experiences. A *balance* of young adult fiction and the classics is what I propose.

WHY WRITE THIS BOOK?

This brings me to the main purpose in writing this book: to offer alternatives to the ways in which young adult literature is used in upper elementary and lower secondary classrooms. This purpose has two foci: (1) the selection of texts and (2) the ways in which they are taught. First, while there are many teachers who encourage wide reading of young adult books, few choose to use them for serious literary study. Although many young adult novels do not have the qualities that bear the kind of scrutiny that literary study involves, some do lend themselves well to interpretive study as *literary* works. It is from these that representative texts will be drawn on for discussion throughout this book. Second, where I have seen young adult books used in classrooms (e.g., Cormier's *The Chocolate War* [1974] or O'Brien's *Z for Zachariah* [1974]), they are mostly taught with the same kind of focus that classical works receive: that is, what the plot is, who the main characters are, what *the theme* is, which point of view the author used, and so on. They are often accompanied by questions that test comprehension rather than questions that encourage interpretive exploration and push students to consider the books from a perspective different from the one that influenced their first response to them. I have also seen students in these settings struggle to find the "right answer" and to lose their connections with the books as well as their confidence as readers. Always framing the teaching of literature in schools is the larger, long-term goal of encouraging students to become lifelong readers of literary texts. We know that many students are alienated from literature as a result of their school experiences as readers, that they are often frustrated by their failure to "get what the teacher wants," and that they are often alienated by selections that reflect adult values that do not serve well as bridges from adolescent to adult worlds (Grossman, 1990).

FRAMING ALTERNATIVE APPROACHES
TO TEACHING YOUNG ADULT FICTION

In considering all the critical theories currently available, we could approach a literary text from one or more of four dimensions or perspectives (Figure 1.1): view relative to reader, view relative to context, view relative to text, and view relative to author. These categories are not new (see Abrams's discussion of orientations of critical theories in his seminal work, *The Mirror and the Lamp* [1953]; but I am also indebted to James Phelan [personal communications, 1997] for his application of Abrams's theory). The actual placement of the various types of criticism is a personal extension of that model. Whatever perspective is adopted is ultimately attributable to the way in which we *position* ourselves as *readers* of the text. As I have stated elsewhere (Soter & Letcher, 1998), "selecting any kind of literary theory is just like selecting a literary text for study: much depends on what our goals are" (p. 25).

Nevertheless, the four dimensions referred to above are definable, and they result in very different ways of reading the texts; assume very different values relative to the text, context, readers, and writers; and ask us to consider quite different questions as we engage in the interpretive act. At the same time, these dimensions are not unrelated to one another. Overlaps are the rule rather than the exception. A brief description of each follows.

View Relative to the Reader

If we approach the text from the perspective of readers, we invite and acknowledge the play of subjectivity in the interpretive act. Indeed, some would argue that any approach to the text could be considered a reader response. Essentially, a view of the text relative to the reader sees the reader

FIGURE 1.1. Ways of Viewing Literary Text: Positioning of the Reader

View Relative to the Reader e.g., Reader Response Criticism	View Relative to the Context e.g., New Historicism
View Relative to the Text e.g., New Criticism	View Relative to the Author e.g., Autobiographical Criticism

Notes. Literary theories may also reflect two or more of these views; for example, New Rhetorical Criticism may combine views relative to the text as well as to the author and the reader; feminist criticism may combine views relative to the reader, the author, and the context. Thus, locating a literary theory within a particular view is always somewhat arbitrary and open to interpretation.

This model is based on Abrams's (1953) extensive discussion of critical theories and the orientations that they reflect, although it is a necessarily simplified rendering of that complex discussion. I am also indebted to James Phelan's advice (personal communication, 1997) in developing this model as a workable image to help students understand the notion that criticism is, indeed, a form of orientation. An earlier version of this model is published in Soter & Letcher (1998).

as responding to the text according to his or her cultural, social, and personal orientation and history. The subjectivity of the reader may be perceived as socially and culturally situated, but the primary critical interest is in why and how the reader responds to the text. Thus, depending on the subjective orientation of the reader, we might consider the text from a psychological response perspective, a social/cultural perspective, or, perhaps, from a feminist perspective. Whatever the critical lens, however, the focus is on the reader's stance relative to the text.

View Relative to the Context

In the slippery ground between reader and author lies the content of the text as well as the perspective in which that content is delivered. Cultural criticism (and one of its precursors, New Historicism) perceives text as grounded in the larger social and cultural context occupied by both authors and readers. Literary texts are not necessarily seen as separate from other kinds of texts, but they are examined in terms of being products of a particular time, place, and zeitgeist (philosophical orientation). Marxist criticism would go further and see literary texts (and all texts) as "units of production"—that is, as products of an economic and political structure. Cultural studies, which emerged from cultural criticism, for example, have moved readers, writers, and texts into the larger sociocultural contexts that both *create and are created by them.* "In fact," observes Rogers (1997), "literature study is increasingly viewed as the study of culture . . . because literary texts are . . . cultural texts and because readers read from various cultural positions" (p. 97). Leitch (1992) argues that "for good or ill, literary criticism and literature *are cultural* in the sense that they share in the regimes of reason operative in societies" (p. 1). Embedded in the cultural critical position is also, however, the view that literature itself is no more than one of the many manifestations of human activity. "Literary works," states Leitch (1992), "are increasingly regarded as communal documents or events with social, historical and political dimensions rather than as autonomous artifacts within an aesthetic domain" (p. ix). As such, literature and literary criticism are as much a reflection of ideologies as are any other texts. Seen from this view, even an insistence that literary texts should be viewed only as aesthetic artifacts is a view steeped in ideology.

View Relative to the Text

In adopting a view of reading literature from a textual perspective, we focus on close scrutiny of textual elements in order to understand better how they work to bring about the artistic unity of the work. We are also interested in understanding how the text affects us the way it does. It is difficult to imagine divorcing oneself from the concept of "effect" on readers, but this is precisely what early New Critics asserted as necessary in the task of critical analysis. Authorial intention and possible effects on readers are excluded from this kind of analysis (Wimsatt & Beardsley, 1954). Underlying this view of literary text is the assumption that it is a "public" text, defined by "what public norms of language allow [the text] to mean"; thus, "the text's aesthetic success or failure must be judged by those terms alone" (Richter, 1989, p. 727). Although other formalist critics such as Crane (1953), Richards (1929), and Shlovsky (1990) acknowledged the "literariness" of literary language, Russian formalists generally saw texts as "representations of reality as a technique for defamiliarizing the social ideas of the dominant culture, and thus for challenging our automatic acceptance of those ideas" (Richter, 1989, p. 723). That is, literary text is seen as a self-contained system and, according to New Critics, literary language is a specialized kind of language.

Neo-Aristotelian critics, however, depart from this narrow view of literary texts as independent of those who create them as well as of those who read them through their concern with both authorial intention and readers' responses to that intention. For this reason, they occupy a midpoint between the world of the author and the world of the text (Figure 1.1). Close textual analysis is central to neo-Aristotelian criticism, but only in terms of asking how elements of the literary text, particularly narrative techniques, have an effect upon the reader.

View Relative to the Author

In adopting this view of the text, we would focus on rhetorical strategies employed by the author, assuming (rightly or wrongly) that the author has some intention in utilizing those strategies as a way of affecting readers. We might also consider the text as autobiographical and seek to see in it evidence of authorial states of mind or stances adopted by the author in relation to morality; ethics; or political, cultural, and social issues. This view does not see the text as "innocent" (that is, without a guiding intention) but rather as a deployment of the author's perspective on life-related issues that, in turn, are reflected in what is written and how it is written. Neo-Aristotelians, for example, as did Aristotle, perceive texts as designed to achieve certain effects and purposes—for example, tragedy is designed to elicit pity and fear in order to bring about catharsis in the receiver of the "text" (whether oral or written).

Figure 1.1 is, I agree, a simplification of what is really a complex overlapping of a plethora of critical perspectives and practices now available to us. However, representing such perspectives and practices as *orientations toward literature* will, I believe, enable students to better understand the *nature and purposes* of such critical perspectives and practices. That is, there is no mysterious ordination involved in adopting one perspective or another—the latter *is* a result of how we view literary texts and their purposes. I have also provided a grouping of the range of critical perspectives available to us according to whether or not a particular perspective preceded or superseded structuralism (Figures 1.2 and 1.3). As readers consider these groupings and their various manifestations, I invite them to locate the perspectives in one or more of the four quadrants identified in Figure 1.1. This cross-referencing will have a bearing in later chapters in which individual perspectives will be used as lenses through which to view a particular young adult novel.

SELECTED CRITICAL PERSPECTIVES

Stevens and Stewart (1992) describe the way we might approach the study of literature as "simply the method one uses to find answers to questions about literature, and [that] each [of us] must decide what questions can be legitimately asked about literary texts and what method is likely to be effective in answering them" (p. 7). This is a useful starting point for de-

FIGURE 1.2. Prestructuralism and Structuralism: Representative Critics

Traditional Historical Criticism	This criticism is concerned with questions of origin and influence (e.g., Renaissance, Early Modern Studies, Romanticism, etc.). It focuses on qualities of the language of literature relative to historical, social, economic, and cultural developments. Works are examined in light of what they reflect of a period. [Aggeler, Gittings, Lovejoy, Mathew, Monk, Spiller, Tillyard]
Aristotelian poetics	This involves the analysis of literature in terms of what makes a message a work of art: its principles of construction and how the technique and structure of a text create a specific effect. [Aristotle, Crane, Halliwell, Olson, Sacks]
Russian formalism	This involves the notion of literature as consciously constructed to achieve special effects, whether "natural" or "aesthetic." Russian formalists, however, were more interested in the structure of the literary text and contended that human content (emotions, ideas, reality) had no significance in itself but rather provided a context for the functioning of literary devices. Critics also made distinctions between the literary and the nonliterary. [Bakhtin, Jakobson, Propp, Shlovsky, Tomashevsky]
New Criticism	This perspective could be described as anti-intentional formalism. The meaning of the text is seen to reside in the words and structures of the text alone. Literature is seen as a special kind of language concerned with the emotive realm. [Brooks, Krieger, Ogden, Richards, Wimsatt, Beardsley]
Structuralism/ semiotics	As a movement, structuralism seeks to explain and understand texts as cultural phenomena. Signs and what they signify (e.g., literary texts, poems, menus) are socially and culturally constructed. Meaning can be inferred through analyzing structures inherent in such texts in terms of their binary oppositions and the implied relationships these structures have with each other within a semantic hierarchy. Such analysis is possible because structuralists see binary oppositions as stable within the formal structures that frame them. [Barthes, Culler, Eco, Saussure, Todorov]

FIGURE 1.3. Poststructural Developments: Deconstruction and Related Perspectives and Critics

Deconstruction	The central notion is the indeterminancy of any truth whether expressed in literary or nonliterary texts. There is no neutrality or objective truth either in the reader or in the text or in the social/cultural systems from which these spring. Assigned meaning is seen as privileged, never innocent; established hierarchies are reversed and new hierarchies are displaced. Indeterminancy prevails. [Culler, de Man, Derrida, Miller]
Feminism and gender studies	Feminist and gender studies are concerned with the socially and culturally situated nature and function of women in the world as represented in literature. Feminist critics focus on how women write and read literary text, how and why women resist male-gendered texts, and how they view traditional roles of women as a result of exploitation in patriarchal societies. Feminist criticism is not a rigidly defined methodology but a general orientation toward the literary experience, using a variety of existing critical techniques for its own purposes. [Cixous, Fetterley, Kristeva, Mitchell, Showalter]
Psychoanalytic criticism	A critical perspective influenced by Freudian and Jungian and Lacanian psychoanalysis. If Freudian, the focus is on the work as representative of Oedipal articulations on the part of the author. If Jungian, it involves the analysis of a work of art in terms of archetypes. Lacanian criticism focuses on a reinterpretation of Freud through language. [Bettleheim, Dillon, Frye, Holland, Kristeva, Lacan, Smith]
New Historicism	New historicists reject the view that literary text is an object of history and emphasizes, instead, that we read it in terms of present values and attitudes. It is basically a critical perspective that sees all texts as products of social and cultural systems, thus minimizing the role of the individual author in its production, and denies that literary text is distinct from other kinds of texts. [Greenblatt, Hunt, Michaels, Montrose, Morris]
Cultural studies	These critics see texts, writers, and readers embedded in cultural contexts that frame their creation and interpretation. Reading literary texts depends on the cultural and literary conventions and practices we have acquired and, in essence, is a co-construction of those texts. [Bakhtin, Baudrillard, Eagleton, Foucault, Girard, Hodge, Lyotard, Said]
Ethnic/ Postcolonial criticism	This perspective challenges traditional ideas about the canon, which works deserve serious attention, and questions established approaches to critical practice on the grounds that these distort our understanding of representative literary text. Ethnic/postcolonial critics argue that works representative of other cultures must be culturally situated, as must critical practice, in order to appropriately evaluate them. [Ashcroft, Bhabba, Boelhower, Davis, de la Garza, Gates, Griffiths, hooks, Minh-ha, Rivera, Said]
Rhetorical Studies	Rhetorical Studies emerged with the later generation of Aristotelian Critics. It involves the study of why a work of art affects us the way it does and takes into account the role of the reader and the positioning of the reader relative to the author's manipulations of the text. [Booth, Phelan, Rabinowitz, Rader]
Reader Response/ Hermeneutics Phenomenology/ Reception Theory	Reader Response Theories have many different manifestations, but essentially, the text is seen to interact with the reader who brings all his/her experiences (cultural, social, cognitive, emotional, literary, linguistic) to bear in the engagement with the text. A central question in reader response and related theories is "who" is the reader. [Bleich, Fish, Holland, Iser, Jauss, Mailoux, Rosenblatt, Steig, Suleiman]

ciding what approaches we should use. They also clear the way for deciding which approaches might be more valuable than others when they add, "some differences among critical approaches reflect varying interests and emphases" and that "the approaches are not models from which one is to make a choice for emulation" but rather, "they represent the main ways literary critics are thinking and writing about literature at present" (pp. 8–9).

As I discussed in the preceding section, one could approach a literary text from one or more of four viewpoints or foci: view relative to the reader, view relative to the context, view relative to the text, and view relative to the author (see Figure 1.1). At the same time, it might also be helpful to consider the various critical perspectives available to us from a historical framework: prestructuralist and post-structuralist (see Figures 1.2 and 1.3). Although structuralism is a type of formalist criticism, it was not concerned with individual texts so much as with literary systems—that is, the codes and conventions of human communication in general, of which literary systems are but one of the "sciences of signs" (Strickland, 1981, p. 13). In grouping the critical perspectives as pre- and poststructuralist, I am obviously using structuralism as a marker and suggesting that ways in which literary theorists approached the practice of criticism shifted significantly at about the time that structuralism began to emerge in critical analyses. Structuralism heralded the end of the kind of formalist criticism that asserted literary text and language as distinct from ordinary language. As Birch (1989) points out, the Romantic notion of the text as an organic whole, having intrinsic unity and, hence, intrinsic meaning, did "not permit speculation of anything other than the meaning inherent in the text" (p. 66). One branch of structuralism still saw "language as a self-contained, unique coherent system" (p. 66), but the fundamental concept of structuralism— that "the world is made up of relationships rather than things" (Hawkes, 1977, p. 17)—also contained the seeds of poststructuralist criticism, which is largely based on the notion that "man constructs the myths, the social institutions, virtually the whole world as he perceives it, and in so doing, constructs himself" (Hawkes, 1977, p. 14). Structuralism opened the door for those competing views of language, and among its vehicles, texts (including literature) would subsequently come to be perceived as social and cultural constructs (inventions, if you will) rather than as absolutes.

Prestructuralism and Structuralism

Traditional Historical Studies of literature viewed the literary text as a product of an author located in a particular time and place. However, although this perspective suggests links with later cultural critical perspectives that place the literary work as a product of a particular place and time in history, the link ends there. Traditional Historical Studies saw text as reflective of the social and political contexts of the time. Cultural Studies sees the text as a *product among other products* of a particular time and place. In other words, the literary text as object is essentially no more significant than any other object. All objects, in effect, become cultural artifacts. Given this perspective, we could, arguably, rename the study of literature as the study of culture.

The primary characteristic of much prestructuralist criticism was an attention to the formal properties of literary text. At the same time, attempts to remove the involvement of writers and readers from textual analysis often appear artificial in retrospect. This was, nevertheless, what New Critics insisted upon as sound critical practice.

Structuralists also "exclude the *actual* author and *actual* reader from the textual level of the narrative" (Selden, 1989, p. 65; emphases added). Instead concepts such as "narrator" and "implied reader" (among others) are used in discussion of the relationships among authors, texts, and readers. Further, "binary oppositions" (e.g., feminine/masculine; high/low; hot/cold, etc.) are "fundamental to structuralist thought" (Selden, 1989, p. 55). Another basic assumption among structuralists is the reduction of all narratives to three basic or essential structures, identifiable through the following dimensions: thematic; linear (plot); and how the narrative is communicated, or what is termed "the structure of narration" (Selden, 1989, p. 63). In practical terms, the latter refers to a formulation that may or may not have the following elements: actual author–implied author–narrator/narratee–implied reader–actual reader (Selden, 1989, p. 64). However, as noted earlier, the actual author and actual reader are not factored into an interpretation of the literary work.

All the prestructuralist critical perspectives (see Figure 1.2) share the notion of the literary text as bound by intrinsic structures that readers are able to perceive through close study of the text. That is, literary language is a self-contained system that assumes, in effect, an *ideal reader*, one who is able to decode the "language of literature" (Hawkes in Birch, 1989, p. 126). However, as implied in an earlier section in this chapter, structuralism embodied the seeds of its undoing, for readers can only make sense of the intrinsic structures of a text through an extensive knowledge of how texts come to mean what they do to us. That knowledge, in turn, is not gained in isolated situations but through learning what texts mean to others. We learn to decode texts in relation to how others decode them. Indeed, we are *taught* how to decode them appropriately. As structuralists have generally claimed, systems and their signs are constructs and implicit in this claim are the social and cultural contexts that construct them. Thus, if we accept that systems and their signs are products of our socially and culturally mediated perceptions, we can no longer regard them as fixed, for the notion of fixed, closed systems and their signs can only survive if we assume ideal, rather than real readers. This, in turn, means that if we can construct meaning, so can we un-construct, de-construct, and re-construct meaning.

Poststructuralism, Deconstruction, and Related Perspectives

As implied in the preceding discussion, the stability of the meaning embodied in two central concepts in structuralism—the "signifier" (or encoded symbol) and its relationship to the "signified" (or the objective concept signified)—was challenged in the 1960s by early poststructuralists, who questioned the predictable nature of their functioning. Simply put, all utterances, whether spoken or written, are open to an unidentifiable number of interpretations depending on many factors, including time, place, speaker(writer), listener(reader) and the nature(s) of their relationships and the contexts (both broad and narrow) in which they function.

As a result, Selden (1989) notes that poststructuralists "totally rejected the assumptions of traditional literary criticism" (p. 76). In practical terms, this means that nothing can ever be identified as an absolute meaning. What seems may not be what is. We could take Avi's *The True Confessions of Charlotte Doyle* (1990) as a useful example of a poststructuralist fiction in that throughout the novel the author plays with us in terms of whether or not the *confessions* are indeed confessions or whether they are merely fictions written by a manipulative, histrionic young woman. On the other hand, one could view the text just as easily as a sociohistorical account of a young woman's struggle to survive in what, to her, was an entirely alien context, and thus take the novel at face value. Selden (1989) terms this the "doubleness of the whole process of an individual's identity" (p. 79).

Given the shift from the *determinacy* of text, critics also became interested in the *indeterminacy* (see Figure 1.3 for representative perspectives) of other aspects of reading literary text, including assumed roles and relationships of authors, texts, and readers. Once taking this path, it was not a stretch to question even the nature of the act of reading (e.g., as in feminism, postcolonialism, psychoanalytic reader response criticism, and more recently, gay criticism (Queer Theory). Critics introduced concepts such as "resistance" (Jauss, 1982; Fetterley, 1978) and the possible role of the subconscious in readers. Indeed, one could argue that many poststructuralist critics have seen their role as being to "disrupt other people's discourses and knowledge" (Selden, 1989, p. 93).

The extreme end of poststructuralism, which tends toward an endless discussion of what the text may or may not mean (as some of us see its most formalist strand, deconstruction) and, in turn, how impossible it really is to define anything, seems to be leading to a shift in criticism as more critics in the past decade or so dare to suggest that they are either anti-deconstruction or that this manifestation of it is "dead" (Ellis, 1989; Kaplan, 1988). The shift from what we know as the "modern" period (intellectual thought from approximately the late 18th to the late 19th century) to the postmodern may be said to be marked by poststructuralism and the most obvious manifestation of it, deconstruction. Poststructuralists also attend to the binary oppositions of structuralists, but they do so in order to dismantle the hierarchies they see embedded in them (e.g., man/woman, white/black, child/adult, and so on). This practice reflects a belief in the ideological nature of *all* discourse—thus, the purpose of dismantling conceptual hierarchies in texts is to *expose* their ideological nature. These concepts are well illustrated in Paul de Man's (1989) essay "Semiology and Rhetoric," in which he argues:

> Literature as well as criticism—the difference between them being elusive—is condemned (or privileged) to be forever the most rigorous and, consequently, the most unreliable language in terms of which man names and modifies himself. (p. 1021)

The admission of "indeterminacy" as a concept related to reality and its manifestations in "objects" such as language is also an admission that social and cultural factors might influence how we interpret those "objects"—considerations that are central concerns in what has come to be known as "cultural criticism." One could argue that feminism and postcolonial criticism as well as New Historicism are manifestations of cultural criticism. As we shift about to find new categories and new labels for rethought categories, we could become mired in a morass of meaningless "meanings," and, thus, I bring us back to the four quadrants I presented in Figure 1.1 and suggest that whatever our perspectives, we could try to locate them in one or more of those four quadrants. That being said, the *suggested* grouping of the critical perspectives in Figures 1.2 and 1.3, are *re-presented* in Figure 1.1 as reflecting various "views" of the text relative to the reader, the context, the text, and the author. My students have found the latter more helpful than the former listings as we decide which of the novels *invite* us to consider them from one perspective rather than another. We make that choice depending on how we *perceived* that invitation.

YOUNG ADULT FICTION SELECTIONS

I now turn to introducing the young adult novels to be discussed in each of the chapters and the critical perspectives that appeared to be a natural choice for my discussion of each. Were I to reread the novels in some future period, I have no doubt that I might view them through another critical lens. Each time I read these works new insights emerge, but this is the nature of reading and rereading. For the present, however, each novel is discussed from one critical perspective on the basis, I like to think, of an invitation issued by the text itself. The novels and the frames through which I view them include the following: Gary Paulsen's *The Island* (1988) from a mythological/psychological perspective; Cynthia Voigt's *Homecoming* (1980) from a feminist perspective; James and Christopher Collier's *My Brother Sam Is Dead* (1974) from a New Historicist perspective; Vera and Bill Cleaver's *Where the Lilies Bloom* (1969) from a rhetorical perspective; Avi's *The True Confessions of Charlotte Doyle* (1990) from a deconstructive perspective; and Walter Dean Myer's *Somewhere in the Darkness* (1992) and Shizuko Go's *Requiem* (1985) from a cultural response perspective. In the final chapter of the book, I explore links between response and criticism through a discussion of readers' responses to a selection of young adult novels that have been used in my courses. I include this discussion because I believe that, unlike what we might *wish* to believe on college campuses, our primary task in teaching literature in schools is to bring about *engaged reading*, and in order to do that we must *begin* with the reader and *not* with the text. In this way we also create the bridge that enables student readers to walk back and forth from the world of the reader toward and into the worlds of the text, the author, and the contexts that contain readers, texts, and authors.

Within each chapter, the reasons for my reading the novels from a particular perspective are given, as well as a discussion of each from that perspective. Various ways of working with the novels (e.g., classroom activities, questions and/or assignments) will also be suggested, though many others would also be possible. As I explored ways in which these novels could be approached, some activities worked with some of my classes and not with others. Therefore, they are meant to serve only as *examples* of how to explore the critical perspectives, with the caution that they are *no more than that*. Finally, I always return my own classes to one main question before selecting either a critical approach or a range of classroom activities to go with it. That question is: *What do I want my students to learn from this experience*?

That question, in turn, serves as a lodestar for other related ones such as: Which critical perspective will enable us to accomplish that learning goal? Why and how? Which activities and assignments seem to work best for which goals? For example, do I want my students to explore a novel from a particular critical perspective, or do I primarily want them to know *how to read* from that perspective? Alternatively, how might the application of a critical perspective enable me to evaluate what they have learned from the experience?

As stated earlier, questions like these bring us back to the larger goals embedded in the question: Why teach literature at all? Among those larger goals are to enable students to expand the culture of the home—to broaden the world they know; to value literature, especially culturally designated "great" literature; and to contribute to the emotional, spiritual, and intellectual growth of the individual (Purves, Rogers, & Soter, 1995).

Balancing these goals in terms of novels we select and, therefore, encourage our students to select will hopefully make the teaching of literature a more engaging experience for them.

My desire to influence patterns of why and how we teach literature in schools, particularly young adult literature, is reflected in the content of this book—a range of alternatives to how literature is used in the classroom. In the process, I hope teachers will also consider their *own acts of reading*, getting in touch with who they are as readers, what influences them as readers, and how their histories as readers inform and influence their present practices as teachers of literature. I believe these questions must be explored if we are to begin our *own charting of critical waters*—as we must do with many young adult novels.

I hope that in describing my own journey as well as those of my students as "navigations" in formerly uncharted waters, I am offering a way of thinking about literary theory and its place both in the school setting and in relation to a body of literature that is still relatively untouched by formal critical analysis in a way that will not undermine the power of the initial engagement with these texts. I see the act of interpreting literary texts from any critical perspective as *raising more questions than answers* about those texts, and with the patience and grace of my readers in mind, I followed this pattern in my discussions of the novels. Therefore, I hope readers will see my applications of critical perspectives to the selected young adult novels as *exploratory*, as *indicative of possibilities*, rather than as authoritative versions or interpretations. In each case, my reading comes from my own initial encounter with the texts, establishing a dialogue, as it were, with the text, inviting the text to "speak" to me and allowing me to "speak" to the text. The result is *a kind of dance*, the lead dependent on multiple factors that work on both readers and texts. As I explore the young adult selections from a perspective that emerged as a result of my own interaction with the text, I am also reminded that I can speak only for *my own reading*, not that of others.

CHAPTER 2

Psychological Criticism: Motives, Quests, and Inner Selves in The Island

I could see the heron in all things the heron was, without seeing me at all, and it changed me, made me look at things that way, made me see in a new way and, finally, made me look at myself in a new way.

(Paulsen, 1988, p. 52)

DIMENSIONS OF PSYCHOLOGICAL LITERARY THEORY

Psychological criticism, says Steven Lynn (1990), is "in its most common-sensical form, an . . . approach to a text [that] involves focusing attention on the motivations and relationships involved in both the writing and reading of that text" (p. 108). According to Lynn, the mental processes of authors, characters, and/or readers are in focus. A psychological approach to literature is not new; one could argue that it has existed as long as we have asked questions like "Why do characters act the way they do?" or "What are the intentions of the writer in this work?" These questions are typical of a rhetorical orientation toward texts in that they direct attention to ways in which authors manipulate texts to evoke particular effects on readers. They also reflect a desire to know and understand motive, a question that goes beyond the text. According to Lacan, motive can only be retrieved by "re-creating" the text "according to readers' own inner landscapes" and as part of readers' pursuit to seek answers to their own identities through something like a work of fiction (quoted in Cuddon, 1991, p. 359).

Psychological criticism probably owes its birth to the work of Freud, who sought to discover connections between artists and what they actually create. In literature, this results in an analysis of characters as invented by the authors, as well as a study of the language these characters use and the imagery related to them and their actions. Freudian critics, like Edmund

15

Wilson and Lionel Trilling, thus explored relationships between the "wound" of a childhood experience in the artist's life (Cuddon, 1991, p. 357) and both the artist's creation and the nature of his creativity. Others, such as Erik Erikson (1963), investigated the assumed relationship between a poet's mind and what he writes. Still others extended Freud's concept of Oedipal envy through studies of how the oedipal complex surfaces in relation to the poets, assumed as oppressed by the work of past great poets and, thus, standing in relation as son to them. In this scenario, the younger poet sees the older ones as rivals and is ridden by guilt as well as hate, envy, and anger as he feels both compelled to reject and rebel against his "fathers while suffused with love and admiration for them" (Cuddon, 1991, p. 357).

Post-Freudian psychoanalytic criticism also surfaced in reader response theories (Bleich, 1978; Holland, 1975, 1980). Influenced by Freudian rather than Lacanian theories, Holland argued that readers seek to see themselves in the literary texts and that their search for unity in the text is a reflection of what he termed personal "identity themes" (1980, p. 121). Consequently, readers reconstruct the work to fit the pattern of their own "defensive" and "adaptive strategies" (1980, p. 125). According to Selden (1989), they might also discover in the work "fantasies which gratify [them]" (p. 110). Ultimately, post-Freudian critics believe readers "transform the work from the level of crude gratification to the level of aesthetic or philosophical unity" (quoted in Selden, 1989, p. 110). Thus, the identity theme influences how the text is read. That is, depending on the philosophical, ethical, and emotional orientations of readers, each could generate quite different meanings of the text that, in turn, would reflect their underlying values. The primary intention, however, is still to understand the text and what it "means."

In contrast, David Bleich's subjective criticism (1978) argues that the intent of the reader is to make the text serve as a means of understanding him- or herself. If there is any objectification in the reader's response, it is through that reader's explanation of that response—that is, what generated it and how it was framed, but only in relation to the reader. The meaning of the text is always perceived as a meaning framed by a reader's personal history and all that this entails.

Departing from a Freudian perspective, Carl Jung's archetypal criticism argued that "the literary work is not the focus for the writer's or reader's personal psychology but a representation of the relationship between the personal and collective unconscious, the images, myths, symbols, archetypes of past cultures" (Selden & Widdowson, 1993, p. 137). Fundamental aspects of the human experience are perceived as archetypal within this construct: birth, death, aging, growing up, love, family, community or tribal life, intergenerational struggles, fraternal rivalries. Also within this frame, certain character types emerge as archetypal: the hero, the villain, the victim, the self-made man, the femme fatale, the wanderer, and so on. Everything, potentially, has symbolic, archetypal significance, although certain symbols carry more weight than others, depending on their currency over past eras; for example, crosses, circles, the number 3, and colors, as well as various animals such as eagles, snakes, owls, lions, and hares. According to this view (Cuddon, 1991) rituals such as rites of passage, fertility rites, and redemptive rituals influence the plot structure and its evolution and have thematic significance.

More recently, poststructural psychoanalytic criticism has been influenced by the work of Jacques Lacan (see Sarup, 1992, for a detailed discussion of Lacan's theories and their influence on poststructuralist critical theories). Very briefly, while Lacan did not disagree with Freud's view of the influence of the subconscious in terms of how we perceive reality, he departed from Freud in viewing that influence as always disrupted by the influence of language, or discourse. Selden and Widdowson (1993) describe it as a process in which the "I" is lost to itself through a process of "substitutions," which could include externally derived roles such as "son" or "daughter" or "father" or "mother." That is, if there is an intrinsic sense of oneself as distinct from any other individual and as distinct from the contexts within which we are also defined, that sense of self is always deconstructed or overturned, as it were, by how we are defined by our social and cultural roles through the language we use to describe them. Furthermore, they argue that these signifiers or terms may be substituted by others, depending on how the "I" perceives itself in relation to others who have also entered into the symbolic order. Language is not stable, and, hence, neither is what we consider and define as reality. Fundamentally, we are shaped by the social and cultural context in which we find ourselves; and within that context, we (as subject positions) shift in accordance with what Lacan termed the "floating preexisting system of signifiers which take on meanings only within a language system" (quoted in Selden & Widdowson, 1993, p. 138).

Although I have taken some space to describe the influence of Lacan, the slippery ground that his theories imply may be developmentally inappropriate for students in middle and lower secondary school. Most of these have yet to identify what they consider reality and are themselves in a constant process of self-definition in relation to their growing perceptions of the social and cultural systems that surround them. However, the Lacanian view of reality may have much to say to the naturally unstable situation in which adolescents find themselves.

GARY PAULSEN'S *THE ISLAND*: A SYNOPSIS

Unlike many of Paulsen's young adult novels, *The Island* (1988) is not an adventure story where the main character faces challenges from the external world, overcomes them, and learns something about himself and others in the process. The journey and adventure is primarily an *internal* one. The novel opens with an unmarked chapter describing the island that becomes the place in which Wil finds himself. Paulsen leaves no doubt in readers' minds that he intends us to see this island as significant when he explicitly declares the link between Wil Neuton, the protagonist, and the island within the first few pages of the novel.

Fifteen-year-old Wil Neuton and his family leave Madison, Wisconsin, one summer because of his father's promotion, moving to the smaller community of Pinewood in the northern part of the state. Perceived through Wil's eyes, this move is little different from others that had been proposed throughout his life—potentially disastrous. Nevertheless, the family moves because they must or his father will lose his job. Wil sees his life ruined. He will leave a familiar and manageable town, friends, places to eat and hang out, and a place in which he knows how to avoid those he wants to avoid.

As Susan, a girl he befriends, says, "Pinewood has one of everything. . . . One church, one bar, one grocery store, one dime store, one hardware store, one gas station, one school" (p. 59). When Wil's family arrives in Pinewood, there is initially little opportunity to make new friends. Wil sets out to explore the surrounding area as much for something to do as for any other reason. He stumbles across a lake in the middle of which is an island. Almost as if it was meant to be, he finds a wooden boat lying near where he stopped his bicycle. The boat, though old, is still intact, and Wil follows an instinct that nudges him to take it out onto the lake and toward the island. The rest of the novel focuses on Wil's inner journey as he comes to learn who he is in relation to animals on the island, to his deceased grandmother, and, finally, to his parents. Wil finds out who he is by discovering who he is not.

THE ISLAND FROM A PSYCHOLOGICAL PERSPECTIVE

Perhaps my own socially and culturally constructed identity responded to what I saw as having symbolic significance in Paulsen's introduction to this novel: namely, an unmarked chapter consisting entirely of a description of an island. Whatever internally prompted me to read this description as having archetypal significance, it was reinformed by the *placement* of this description, which resulted in my perceiving it as having a framing function for all the subsequent developments in the novel. Islands typically suggest images of separation, isolation, and insulation. We often refer to them as havens, places of escape, and places where we imagine ourselves free to be whoever we think we truly are. I found it natural, therefore, to see Wil's emotional and psychological growth an outcome of his increasing intimacy with the creatures on the island as well as the island environment in general. It is only while on the island that he discovers his poetic and artistic self. It is only through his relationship with the island and its animal inhabitants that he learns to see beyond the surface of things and to perceive a unity between himself and them. Paulsen's spiritual connection to the natural world is evident in many of his young adult novels, and I found myself hearing him, rather than his protagonist, in Wil's declaration that "if I can learn a fish, I can learn my father" (p. 200).

As I read the rest of the novel, Paulsen's weaving of excerpts from Wil's journal, Wil's notebook, and a third-person narrator signaled authorial direction—that is, to see beyond the surface construct. We must come to know Wil internally. And what more authentic source is there than a journal in which he writes about what he thinks and reveals his attempts to construct an objective distance from what he sees? I relied on the journal as the truthful account of Wil's feelings about his family, himself, and people he comes to know in the new community. His notebook, however, is a creative workbook of writings and drawings, artistic renderings of Wil's growing astuteness as he observes life around him. Both the journal and the notebook are personal records, but each serves a unique function for the narrative as a whole as well as for Wil. We might ask why Paulsen didn't frame this novel in the first person—why the elaborate three-layered structure? One answer lies in Paulsen's need to have a seemingly objective reality contrasted with Wil's inner reality—something that could not have been achieved had the novel been presented from a single perspective. In reading the novel in this way, the island assumes the function of representing Wil's emerging identity. The seemingly fortuitous circumstances through which he stumbles upon the island, and the seemingly coincidental appearance of a water-worthy boat, can be seen as mechanisms through which Paulsen forces a symbolic connection between the island and Wil's inner development. Should he miss this opportunity, another may not come his way. And so, I found myself drawn to a reading of this novel that resulted in musings about quests, magical places, tests, discoverings—in short, a reading from a psychological (archetypal) perspective.

Wil Neuton: The Archetypal Wanderer

In her revised edition of *The Hero Within: Six Archetypes We Live By*, Pearson (1989) identifies the characteristics of the "Wanderer" (one of six heroic archetypes) as including independence, fear of conformity, exploration of ideas in one's own way, enjoyment of isolated sports, and involvement with the primary life tasks of establishing autonomy, establishing identity, and discovering a vocation. Each reading of *The Island* suggests to me the individual quest of the hero, but it is not a quest to conquer (Pearson's "Warrior"), nor is it a quest that is undertaken with the certainty that the right path is being pursued (Pearson's "Magician"). Rather it is an inner quest, a seeking of self. Others, especially parents and authority figures in general, typically represent what one does not want to be. The Wanderer is essentially a loner, a figure who prefers to reflect rather than undertake battles, to discover why he or she is here in this lifetime, and to honor that discovery if and when it is made. The hero is compelled to seek that identity and purpose despite the conflict and scorn that doing so often generates.

How do I see Wil Neuton fitting this profile? From the very beginning of the novel, Wil is presented as different from his parents, standing out in a way that separates him from them:

> Even at fourteen, Wil Neuton towered over his parents. They were short, and somehow the genes had jumped a generation and made him tall—six feet, two inches—and had given him breadth, a strong body with wide shoulders and long legs and muscled arms with big hands. (p. 5)

As well as being physically set apart, he is also different in terms of what he identifies with:

> Sometimes old wisdom isn't so good. I complained once about household chores and my father told me to sing and act happy when I did them even if I didn't feel that way. That's what his grandfather told him to do. So the next time I edged the side-walk I tried singing "la, la, la" in time with my cutting strokes. As near as I can figure, it didn't help at all. (p. 9)

The difference between Wil and his family, particularly his father, develops and intensifies as Wil begins to spend time on the island, which becomes his sanctuary. As his parents focus on settling the family in their new home, Wil takes a bicycle ride to clear his head. In the process he discovers the island, which is situated in the middle of a lake not far from his new home. It exerts a strong fascination on him and after fortuitously discovering an abandoned boat, Wil rows out to it and explores it for several hours. By the time he leaves, he no longer thinks of Madison or the life he left behind there. He thinks "only of the island, the sunfish, the mallards, the sun, the birds" (p. 23). When he returns and his father asks him where he has been, Wil evades the probe:

> "Just out for a run on the bike. Went farther than I thought I would." Suddenly, for no real reason, he did not want to speak of the island. It wasn't a secret, just a private place, a thing he did not understand yet and he did not want to talk about it. (p. 25)

This journey, this search for self, is akin to the kind of Jungian archetypal criticism that, among other things, asserted a connection between the literary work and the author who produced it, whether consciously or unconsciously. Unlike Frye (1954), who denied a connection between the literary work and its author, I cannot divorce the author from the text. One could even argue that the favorable view we have of Wil is a consequence of Paulsen's need to see his own quests, represented through fiction, in a positive light. Indeed, Wil is close to being a perfect hero figure, although he is clearly fallible. In contrast, Wil's father and, to a lesser extent, his mother and other adults in the novel are all too flawed. Had Paulsen written this novel solely in the first person, I would have perceived this as a natural consequence of Wil's adolescent egocentricity. However, we learn about the adults in the novel from an omniscient narrator outside the action of the novel as well as from Wil's journal and notebook. One wonders, then, whether Paulsen wants to ensure that we read the narrator's seemingly objective account as confirmation of Wil's subjective descriptions of the adults and his feelings about them in his personal writing. Given this scenario, one naturally begins to question Paulsen's motives, subconscious or otherwise, in presenting the characters in this way. Once we move to considering motives, we no longer divorce the author from the text.

Indeed much of Paulsen's fiction reveals a protagonist who needs to find himself, who is consciously separate from others, whether peers or adults, and who cannot discover who he is unless he removes himself from familiar settings and from what threatens him to confirm it. "Wanderers," observes Pearson (1989), "identify a person, an institution, a belief system as the cause of their misery, and then they flee the cause or avoid it" during the first level of wandering (p. 65). The protagonist then must follow a "road of trials," which is marked by tension between "the desire for growth, for mastery, for pushing the limits of one's capacity to achieve versus one's desire to fit in and to please" (Pearson, 1989, p. 68). The ultimate quest *is* to fit in and yet, at the same time, to retain one's own sense of reality as defined by the self as well as by others. Thus, Wil finally is accepted by his parents—his clan—but he can only return when he knows that he can see them for what they are and his place relative to them:

> His father's face was swollen from insect bites and he had a pack with him, a sleeping bag, the binoculars. . . . So sad, Wil thought. Why is this so sad? No, not sad, so . . . so rich. Why is this so rich? Almost too much to stand, what is here, this man who has been watching me, this man—my father. (p. 200)

The clan, as represented in Wil's parents, must accept him as he also now is, as having knowledge and experience that it must value:

> "We didn't know, you see. Didn't understand and maybe we still don't understand." (p. 201)

This is in contrast to their previous perception when his parents first came to visit him on the island:

> "I just want to know if it's drugs." His father held up a hand. "Is it drugs?" (p. 129)

Wil explains that it isn't drugs but meditating:

> "Meditating?"
> "Yes, I sit or stand and do movements and meditate, and it makes my mind blank and clear thoughts come in. . . ." He trailed off as he realized they were both staring at him. His mother's mouth was actually open a bit. . . . His father had a can of pop in one hand and the other frozen on the fliptop. "I mean I realize it sounds kind of crazy . . ." (pp. 129–130)

As Wil digests their response to his attempt to describe what he has been doing on the island, he realizes that he cannot return until he has worked out *for himself* whether or not he is indeed crazy or whether his perception is influenced by theirs. This is Pearson's (1989) *test* in which the Wanderer hero must experience "the emotional crises of learning to trust her own sense of the [other's] reality" (p. 69). The clan (his parents and others) think Wil is mad; Wil thinks he is sane, though he is not at first sure:

> When they were gone, Wil stood a moment, looking across the bay, wondering if there were really something "psychological" about him, a problem he could not know about because if he knew, it wouldn't be a problem— one of those weird things. . . . He was not what he had been before. . . . He

was what he was, and if he was wrong or had mental problems, that was still the way he was, the way he had to live. (p. 132)

This conclusion leads him to focus with renewed energy on his quest, and as he struggles to understand what is going on in himself, the outside world begins to wonder what this boy is doing alone on an island. A camera crew and reporter come to the island seeking a story. After spending several hours with Wil, they leave with the following conclusion:

The spokesman sighed. "It's like she said in the article—kind of incredible. I mean, we're out here taping things and doing things and *we're missing it— missing something.*" To which Wil replied, *smiling*: "Go find an island." (pp. 196–197; emphasis added)

Wil has reached the maturity that awaits the Wanderer at the end of his quest. He is no longer in defiance, nor is he threatened by what the clan represents. He simply sees where he is and where it is. He can create the necessary boundaries that will enable him to honor himself as well as others and "still do what we need to do for ourselves" (Pearson, 1989, pp. 70–71). As Pearson also argues, the Wanderer's quest, while drawing the hero into acknowledging, articulating, and enacting what is initially a *sensed* isolation, leads him or her to a return to his or her community.

Suggestive Structure and Clues to a Mythic Reading

As discussed briefly in the preceding section, Paulsen chose to develop the novel in a three-layered structure: an omniscient narrator who favors Wil; excerpts from Wil's journal, in which he records his thoughts and feelings; and excerpts from Wil's notebook, in which he records his artistic impressions of his family, people in the community, and the life on the island. The notebook entries emerge only after he has visited the island for the first time. Why such a structure, and what does it suggest in terms of Paulsen's motives? The novel opens with the omniscient narrator describing the island in a neutral account of its dimensions and its geological history until Paulsen signals the symbolic weight it will assume throughout the rest of the novel:

From all that time, the small island in almost the exact center of Sucker Lake in the northern part of Wisconsin cannot be known, can only be part of theory and ideas. Hopes. Wishes. Dreams. (p. 3)

From this point it is impossible to read the rest of the novel without making connections between the island and Wil's emergent character at a symbolic level:

But in the summer of the middle of his fifteenth year on earth Wil Neuton discovered the island, or was discovered by the island—he was never sure which—and from that time on it is not necessary to guess about it any longer but only necessary to know Wil. (p. 3)

As the novel progresses, Paulsen maintains a consistent structural pattern: He introduces the chapters with excerpts from Wil's journal, continues the narrative progression through the omniscient narrator, and inserts note-book entries as unmarked chapters. The journal entries reveal a remark-ably mature 15-year-old:

I had an uncle one time who told me life was like a sewing machine, and no matter what you did you couldn't put the thread in it while it was running. Of course he had trouble with drinking so that might not have meant much. I finally figured life isn't like anything. Life is just like life. (p. 67)

Because each journal entry is set at the beginning of each chapter, we cannot help but see it functioning as a frame for the rest of the chapter. It is, at times, an admittedly adolescent voice, but it is also characterized by the kinds of insights one might attribute to an adult who has the benefit of hindsight. Therefore, it was not a significant leap to consider Wil as a idealized projection of Paulsen.

Paralleling the journal entries is the omniscient narrator's account of the other characters in the novel and the action as it evolves. The narra-tor is not, however, unbiased.

As discussed previously in this chapter, Wil "towers" over his parents (suggesting dominance), and through his early journal entries, appears to be endowed with greater wisdom than anyone else around him. His fa-ther does not come off so well:

The first Thursday after school let out for the summer, Wil's father caught both Wil and his mother at the same time in the kitchen before *they* could get away, and he began a conference. He loved to hold conferences, but they tended to be boring in an amiable way, and his wife and son tried to avoid him. (p. 6; emphasis added)

In these few lines we are directed to see Wil and his mother as superior to his father, a view that is confirmed frequently throughout the novel. Wil's father emerges as a man who has never quite achieved his dreams but, more significantly, whose dreams are pathetic rather than admirable:

It wasn't as bad as the time a year earlier when he had come home one after-noon and announced he's come across a plan to raise foxes and retire at forty-

> six. When he started building the cages in the basement and seemed about
> to order the first fox, Wil's mother put her foot down. (p. 7)

Paulsen does not disguise the father–son competition that permeates the
novel. Whether his seemingly detached narrator describes Wil drawing in
his notebook while his father and mother watch "an awful show" (p. 57)
or his parents turning off the television and going to bed at 11 o'clock while
Wil thinks of the island, the result is consistently the same: Wil emerges
as the heroic figure engaged in a serious quest, while his parents, in particular his father, have essentially given up their own quests. By the time
Wil's father asks Wil if he has "gotten involved in some mind of religious
cult" (p. 130) because of his frequent absences from the house, we are
completely on Wil's side. The age-old tables have been turned—the father is outdone by the son and the son now becomes the father's teacher.

Wil's notebook entries, the third parallel structure, provide us with
evidence that he should be taken seriously. He is not simply an adolescent pitted against his father; through his emergent art and writing, he is
pursuing his path to his own salvation, his self-discovery:

> You can't really know it, but only try to know it and that's perhaps what
> living with other people is all about, trying to learn the center of them, learn
> what they are, learn their core when they are in the golden dusty light of a
> kitchen window. (p. 166)

Less obvious, but also apparent, is a subtle shift in the objectively
narrated sections to a style that more closely resembles Wil's own thinking. In the following example, the narrator and the character have not
yet become fused and the narrator is still in the role of omniscient observer:

> Wil was sitting on the right side, and he opened the door and got out, put
> the cat cage down, stretched, then bent over and released Bob, who made a
> straight, gray-hair-line for the small front porch. . . . He had never spent time
> in a cage, never ridden in a truck, never had to move, and apparently, Wil
> judged, didn't think much of any of them. (p. 11)

Contrast this, however, with the example below, in which the line between
Wil and the narrator seems to disappear. The prose rhythms begin to match
the way Wil might have thought and sensed the movements of the heron.
The narrator appears to lose interest in dissembling—he and Wil are very
close:

> Wil leaned back on the rock and lay on his back in the sun and let his mind
> roll. The heron had been something—the way the head had darted to grab
> the frog, and again and again later to take two small fish, minnows really.

> Clean movements, graceful, almost dancing movements, very fast but with almost perfect grace. (p. 49)

By the time we move toward the final pages, the mask is completely off—my sense is that Wil and the narrator *are* one and the same people:

> They were gone now.
>   *And*, he thought, looking at the water by his legs, where the turtle had been, *and how will this turn out?* (p. 199; emphasis added)

We are no longer outside the protagonist's mind as the author moves us into something that resembles his own consciousness imposed on that of the character:

> He went back to the boat and found the notebook and sat with one of the cedar pencils and a blank page, sat staring at nothing, thinking and not thinking—almost being and not being (p. 199)

Given this fusing of narrator with character in what is ostensibly a third-person account, it is difficult to avoid reading the novel autobiographically. Had Paulsen presented the entire account *directly through* Wil's eyes (a first-person account), that might not have occurred to me. But the thinly disguised, objectified narrator paralleled with two first-person intrusions in the forms of the journal and notebook entries suggests that Paulsen is presenting Wil in as many ways as narratively manageable. Why should we see this character from several angles? One possibility is that the strategy forestalls our dismissing Wil's views as too subjective to be worthy of serious consideration. Multifaceted representations enable us to see him from several angles, to develop a fuller sense of his character, and, potentially, to identify with him and to attach our sympathies to his cause.

Although *The Island* has some of the external trappings of other coming-of-age young adult novels, it does invite speculation that Paulsen has been there all along, the author-in-character, Paulsen as he *might* have been rather than as he was—that is, Paulsen as an idealized version of himself. Unlike traditional psychoanalytic criticism, which has typically been interested in *negative* subconscious impulses (e.g., repression, denial, reversal, splitting, regression, sublimation, rationalization), I see Paulsen's projection as positive, as an attempt to explore what had to be brought to consciousness, rather than seeing the fiction as betraying what is subconsciously at work in the author. There is evidence in this novel of tension between portraying parents as they are and, at the same time, "empathizing and honoring another" (Pearson, 1989, p. 71). For the Wanderer to reach his goal, he must be able to "move from dependence to independence, to an autonomy defined in the context of *interdependence*" (Pearson, 1989, p. 72; emphasis added). This is what Wil comes to know when on the lake; "he rowed toward the island" knowing how "this would end":

> It was a high thought, a high and clean and keening thought, as clear as the song the loon made in the slash of moonlight that night on the lake. . . . It would end only when *they* found a bigger island. (p. 202; emphasis added)

APPLICATIONS OF PSYCHOANALYTIC CRITICISM TO OTHER YOUNG ADULT NOVELS

Novels that follow the tradition of the *Bildungsroman* lend themselves naturally to being read from a psychoanalytic perspective. The *Bildungsroman* has as its main focus the psychological and emotional development of the protagonist. Growth takes place as the protagonist faces trials that resemble rites of passage and that result in maturation. Character building is thus central as the hero or heroine accepts responsibility for his or her life and role in the larger social and cultural order. As a romance, the novel will end positively, with the protagonist overcoming obstacles and, in effect, being rewarded in the end with reconciliation or with some other manifestation of triumph. A classic example of the *Bildungsroman* is Brontë's *Jane Eyre* (1847/1960).

Other works of fiction that could be fruitfully explored from a psychoanalytic perspective are those that focus on internal conflicts and motivations of protagonists. John Knowles's *Phineas* (1968) and Robert Cormier's *The Chocolate War* (1974) have protagonists who must deal with self-knowledge and who inquire into motives for acting the way they do. In *Phineas*, protagonists confront truths about themselves and others that invite questions about our own deepest pains. Knowing what it means to be an outsider to peer groups and what cost would be involved if one capitulated in order to be accepted and popular are themes woven through the six stories involved in this collection. In the title story of the collection, self-knowledge comes with shame as the protagonist faces the knowledge that he would never be accused by his friend Phineas, for sending the latter off-balance. The personal journeys taken in the stories of this collection do not yield rewards or cathartic cleansing. Rather, they suggest an author who strips us of any illusions that we might be intrinsically good:

> And then I realized, with relief, that we were equals. He wasn't so unlike me, so peacefully himself, unconscious of conflict and rivalry, after all. He was as vulnerable and treacherous as everybody else (*Phineas*, p. 106)

As another example of the Wanderer myth, Walter Dean Myers's *Somewhere in the Darkness* (1992) offers an interesting parallel to *The Island* of father and son journeys. The father has come to the end of his journey, aware that he has, essentially, failed in his quest. The son is just becoming aware of the role of conscious choice in the selection of his path. He could choose the same path as his father had done and be similarly defeated, or he could choose another path and accept the challenges that he already foresees as part of that choice. We could surmise that the protagonist, Jimmy, chooses the latter, but the ambiguity of the conclusion leaves that as an expressed thought—not action. Time will tell. In this instance, the archetypal struggle between child and parent as competitor will not end when the story ends—Jimmy's quest has just begun, although his reunification with Crab, his father, is the initial call to awakening. By the time Crab dies, Jimmy can no longer return to childhood, illusion is shattered, and he must now face the future as a conscious, choosing being, rather than as a child who can still say "but I did what my parents told me."

Many textbooks about the teaching of young adult literature (e.g., Donelson & Nilsen, 1995) will include chapters on adventure, quest stories, stories that explore the deeper layers of self and the processes by which that self is exposed in order to bring about growth, usually as part of the transition from childhood to adulthood. Not all of these will be of interest for critical study in the ways I've suggested for Paulsen's *The Island*. Even if we agree with Valery's assertion that "no text can ever realize . . . [the] intentions [of an author]" (quoted in Scholes, 1989, p. 54), some texts may invite or suggest a particular critical orientation that may reflect at least some of the author's intentions or motives. One clue that *The Island* could be read from a psychoanalytic perspective lay in its structure, and this may be explored in the suggested activities that follows the present section.

QUESTIONS AND ACTIVITIES FOR FURTHER EXPLORATION

Any attempt to repeat what one teacher has done in one classroom invites at least two possibilities: The first is to limit other explorations and the second is to run the risk of failure in that second classroom. The following applications reflect my own efforts to explore this novel from a psychologically oriented perspective and should be seen merely as examples that may or may not work for someone else. They are also an outcome of *my* readings of the novel, and, as I will suggest again elsewhere, any applications we pursue in our classrooms *will reflect* our own orientations and goals toward both reading literature in general and reading a particular work of literature.

I had stated earlier that the structure of this novel invites speculation about the intentions of the author, so a teacher might want to explore this further by using the following questions and activities.

Questions

1. What polarities and parallels can be perceived in the novel? Some examples include the son rejecting the father, with the father already "castrated" in the eyes of the mute but critical wife/mother; the son's initially close link with his mother compared to his ultimate link with his father; the father's relinquishing his place of authority and, thereby, gaining his son as his "teacher."
2. How are the inner/outer journeys made by Wil Neuton on the island contrasted with his states of being on the mainland? What might the author intend by presenting us with these contrasts?
3. Who speaks for whom, when, and about what in this novel? This type of question focuses on issues of distance from action and variations in distance related to kinds of narration.
4. Why is the action of the novel presented through three different forms? A further question related to this issue might ask students to consider ways in which the entries in Wil's journal versus those in his notebook function as a reflection of narrative roles. Students could then compare and contrast the role of the first-person narrator to that of the pseudo-third-person narrator (what James termed the "third person center of consciousness" [quoted in Booth, 1983, p. 153]). Teachers could further ask students to consider how each of these narrative roles acts as a filter to ensure that readers respond in certain ways to Wil, his family, and those who are shown to not understand what the island represents at a deeper metaphysical level.

Activities

1. Linked to the above questions, teachers could construct dramatized readings in which students take on roles as narrators—reflecting the journal, notebook, and third-person narrator to help students perceive the authenticity of the voices represented by each of these.
2. Following the dramatized readings, students could be asked to explain why they interpreted them the way they did. Alternatively, students could write a defense of their interpretational readings, explaining how they

perceived them to reflect what they thought was going on with Wil and
his quest.

3. Teachers could ask students to conduct textual analysis in an effort to find
   how the author is present even if he appears to have absented himself.
   They could then present a case for their findings on the basis of their textual evidence.

4. More mature students could pursue a Lacanian exploration in which they
   might ask what the text reveals about the repressed unconscious of the
   reader.

5. Alternatively, students could take the role of a school psychologist and
   develop a script that focuses on the psychologist's interview of Wil. This
   would then serve as a basis for discussing how the interview questions
   reveal a certain "reading" of the novel—one that might reflect a particular psychoanalytic orientation on the part of the reader.

This listing of questions and activities that reflect a psychoanalytic
orientation is obviously not exhaustive, but it offers some point of departure for teachers who might wish to explore *The Island* and other possible
texts from this perspective. It has been of interest to me that whenever I
have selected this text for either an undergraduate or a graduate course,
students inevitably drift toward a discussion of quests, archetypal parent–
child conflicts, and questions of motive. Teachers who have used this text
in their middle school classrooms report that their seventh- and eighth-
graders typically focus on similar issues. Could all these communities of
readers be entirely misled, or do they all reflect the influence of an author
who has effectively manipulated his readership to read the text in that way?
As Booth (1983) argues, "we must never forget that though the author
can to some extent, choose his disguises, he can never choose to disappear" (p. 20).

CHAPTER 3

Through a Woman's Eyes: Reading Homecoming *with a Feminist Lens*

A radical critique of literature, feminist in its impulse, would take the work first of all as a clue to how we live, how we have been living, how we have been led to imagine ourselves, how our language has trapped as well as liberated us; and how we can begin to see—and therefore live—afresh.

(Rich, 1972, p. 18)

READING AND WRITING AS A WOMAN

I am not about to condense in a few pages the mass of feminist criticism that is now available. Rather, I have chosen to focus, after a brief discussion of what I see as the main tenets of feminist criticism, on what it means to *read as a woman* in relation *to a text written by a woman*. Male readers in my courses declare confidently that *Homecoming* is a book "for girls." The female readers love it, although they have some concerns about a mother who abandons her children and take to the novel as a testimonial for their younger selves. They see themselves represented in the character of Dicey, and although Voigt departs from the use of a first-person narrator (common in young adult literature), her absent narrator does not attempt to disguise a close affiliation with Dicey, the protagonist of the novel. It seems to be a novel that begs a feminist critique.

Feminist criticism has broadly been concerned with either unearthing, rediscovering, and reevaluating women's writing or with rereading literature from the point of view of a woman (Miller, 1986; Selden, 1989). At the same time, feminists have generally argued that women, as a social class, are exploited by patriarchy at all levels—that is, economincally, politically, and ideologically (Selden, 1989).

These two broad strands of feminist criticism—writing as a woman and reading as a woman—are not in binary opposition to one another. Rather, as one approaches a book written by a woman, one is led to wonder not only about the motives, views, and values of the writer as possibly reflected in the text, but also about oneself in response to that representation of reality. This notion is well captured in Stimpson's (1992) argument concerning the power of the imagination to overcome the limitations created by an imposed male consciousness. Yet as women readers, we may find ourselves struggling to accept what a woman writer identifies as significant or what a woman writer presents as a perspective on the characters and events represented in a text. Perhaps this is an outcome of a lifetime of reading predominantly male texts. Showalter (1977, 1985) argued that "women are expected to identify . . . with a masculine experience and perspective, which is presented as the human one" (quoted in Culler, 1982, p. 51). This is helpful in understanding potential resistance to the representation of reality as perceived by a female writer. According to Culler (1982), Kolodny (1985) claims that "reading is a learned activity which, like many other learned interpretative strategies in our society, is inevitably sex-coded and gender-inflected" (quoted in Culler, 1982, p. 51).

Current feminist criticism presents a rather bewildering array of positions that might be adopted. According to Radford (1992), Kate Millet's feminist reading of D. H. Lawrence as a "critique of male writing" was a turning point in feminist criticism (p. 96). Gender entered discussions of meaning and interpretation and generated rereadings of the canon from the perspective of women. Subsequently, during what Radford (1992) describes as the "second wave of feminist criticism" (p. 96), the focus shifted from reinterpreting male writing through a feminist lens to rereading women-authored texts. Showalter (1977) was particularly influential in the rediscovery of the literature of women as worthy of critical focus at a time when both male and female authors were beginning to be interpreted as "products of the social and political conditions" in which they were being produced (quoted in Radford, 1992, p. 97). In fact, this focus, the hallmark of New Historicist and Marxist critics, was enormously beneficial to feminist criticism in that it validated feminist attention to *how* women write and read and *what* women write and read.

Feminist criticism and more recent postmodern critical perspectives, such as deconstruction and cultural criticism, share the view that meaning is indeterminate; but feminist criticism, notably that of Chodorow (1978) and Gilligan (1982), has also viewed this indeterminacy of meaning from a gendered perspective and sought to use it to liberate women from the constraining influence of the Freudian myth, which argues that women are driven by castration anxiety and thus, "in order to resolve her Oedipal complex, a woman develops abnormally" (Torsney, 1989, p. 185). As Showalter (1977) and Torsney (1989) observed, there is no single feminist critique, but underlying all feminist criticism is the belief that women read, think, and act differently from men.

In applying feminist theory to Cynthia Voigt's novel *Homecoming*, I found myself considering it from two angles: first, reading and writing as a woman, and second, how men and women are situated within the larger social and cultural context and how that, in turn, influences who they are and what drives them to act the way they do. Parts of this reading include responses that students have had to a feminist perspective on the novel. Many of my female students have resisted a feminist reading of *Homecoming*, a response that I found interesting and troubling to my own reading of the novel. I have, therefore, combined the student views with those of my own because this dichotomy illustrates Kolodny's (1985) argument that our reading still reflects the influence of the patriarchal system and its representation of reality. That discussion follows a brief description of the content of the novel.

CYNTHIA VOIGT'S *HOMECOMING*: A SYNOPSIS

A woman abandons her four children in a shopping mall parking lot. The eldest, 13-year-old Dicey Tillerman, is left to decide how she will take care of 11-year-old James, 8-year-old Maybeth, 6-year-old Sammy, and herself. Dicey decides that they have no choice but to make their way to their mother's sister, Aunt Cilla, who lives in Bridgeport, Connecticut. They had all been going there anyway when their mother stopped the car at the mall. There was no point in going back home to Provincetown because their mother would not be there anyway, since she hadn't paid the rent for weeks.

The children eventually reach Bridgeport only to find that their Aunt Cilla had died several months earlier, leaving only Cousin Eunice, a middle-aged, fearful, and timid woman, their only source of protection. Cousin Eunice's plans to adopt the family of four go awry when it seems that Maybeth may be sent to a school for developmentally handicapped children. Dicey decides that the children will seek out their paternal grandmother in Crisfield, Maryland. Reputedly crazy, Abigail Tillerman appears to be their only hope, and Dicey feels they have no choice but to investigate her for themselves. They discover that Abigail Tillerman is not crazy. Rather, she is a strong, idiosyncratic individual who has had to face many challenges, including the loss of two sons and a husband with whom she had a difficult marriage.

The rest of the novel focuses on the children's establishing a relationship with Abigail Tillerman and concludes with her decision to adopt them.

In the process, the children resolve their inner conflicts about their early abandonment by their father, one of Abigail Tillerman's sons. They also come to terms with their mother's mental illness and ultimate death.

HOMECOMING: A FEMINIST READING

Reading and Writing as Women

As with many other young adult novels, we could read *Homecoming* as a coming-of-age tale. Told from Dicey's perspective though the voice of a third-person narrator, the novel is, at one level, about an adolescent's struggles and ultimate growth to maturity through abandonment. Effectively without parents, Dicey takes charge of her siblings and adopts the role of head of the family while seeking a replacement parent figure. In the process, she learns much about herself as well as about others and life in general, resulting in a maturing transformation that we have come to expect in coming-of-age fiction. However, one could also read the novel as a manifesto about women who have been abandoned and marginalized in various ways. It can also be read as a manifesto about how women perceive their relationships with men and how they perceive their roles within a patriarchy. The invitation begins early.

Why did Voigt write a novel that begins with a woman leaving her children? Had the novel been written by a male author, would this opening have been equally arresting to a female reader? Voigt herself does not offer any clues other than that she acknowledged how difficult it was for her to "cook up a reason why a woman would leave her children" and that this was why she had to make the mother in this novel "crazy" (quoted in Garrett & McCue, Vol. 2, 1989, p. 213). According to Voigt, there was "no other conceivable way that a woman could leave her children" (quoted in Garrett & McCue, Vol. 2, 1989, p. 213).

Male students in my courses have not reacted negatively to the image of Liza Tillerman (the mother) abandoning her children in a mall parking lot. Indeed, they do not even comment on it in their journal responses to the novel. On the other hand, female students invariably express both dismay and concern about this opening to the novel. Although they express sympathy for Liza Tillerman, influenced as they are by Voigt's description of her "pale," "sad," "moon-face," they regard the act as unnatural even if they are able to forgive her. Like me, they see this opening and the novel as a whole as a critique of traditional gender roles. And yet, one of my female students resisted the notion that males could not empathetically read this novel *because* it is written by a female author and is about women:

> I continue to struggle with the notion of writing the female experi-
> ence for female readers. I find that, with the exception of childbirth
> and menstruation, males and females may experience many of the
> same emotions, struggles and achievements in their lifetimes because
> we are all human beings. Can a man not feel powerlessness, or fear,
> or pain, or love? Can a man not be nurturing? Can a man not
> identify with Dicey Tillerman? I believe he can.

Does this reading reflect what Bleich (1978) describes as a "rendering of
the reading experience as representative of a general human principle"
and thus, "omitting the subjective immediacy of the experience" (p. 8)?
We know that women have long read male-authored texts resistantly
(Fetterley, 1978), but some of my female students also "read" a feminist
stance on Voigt resistantly. At the same time, some men can and do feel
all the emotions the student mentions in the above comment. What was
interesting was in terms of what was *noticed* and what was not. Fathers
abandoning children (for whatever reason) is not an uncommon scenario
in young adult novels. Mothers abandoning children *is* an uncommon
scenario. Furthermore, if we view *Homecoming* as a critique of traditional
gender roles, some of us may find it difficult to relate to the female characters in it. Several of my female students commented on how generally
unsupportive the women in the novel are; how quite a few of the significant women in it are actually poor caretakers of children; and either how
angry or helpless many of the women appear to be. All of these create
images of women that are in stark contrast to the traditional role of women
as caring mothers and wives.

In this respect, Juliet Mitchell's (1988) proposal that the woman writer
"simultaneously refuses the woman's world and her construction of that
woman's world within a masculine world" (p. 427) is of interest. Liza
Tillerman's actions can be interpreted as a rejection of her "woman's
world," constructed as it is "within a masculine world" (Mitchell, 1988,
p. 427). We could infer that constructing a novel which opens in this way
is evidence of Voigt's subconscious "refusal of the woman's world," since
she has "constructed" that world within "a masculine world," a world that
would condemn a woman who abandons her children no matter how
desperate she is but might accept such an action by a man as at least understandable. Furthermore, Voigt's own struggle as a writer may suggest support for the view of some feminists (Gilbert & Gubar, 1979; Mitchell, 1988)
that "the woman novelist is necessarily the hysteric who wants to repudi-
ate the symbolic definition of sexual difference under patriarchal law, but
is unable to do so because without madness, we are all unable to do so"
(Mitchell, 1988, p. 430). This helps explain why some of my female stu-

dents found it difficult to accept the characters' rejections of their stereo-typical, gendered roles. That is, those students were troubled by what they saw as acts of weakness in the women themselves. However, these students also admitted to the need for subterfuge in order to survive in a patriarchy:

> Dicey is able to succeed in a male-dominated world by employing trickery or cunning. For example, [she] takes advantage of her "boyish" looks in order to fool strangers into thinking that she is a boy. She tells her family that the reason is because it is "safer" to be a boy because then people are less likely to question or trouble them. It seems Dicey is denying that females have power and can handle themselves in any situation. She is also acknowledging and conforming to the idea of a patriarchal society.

While Dicey is not cast as a "hysteric," she is ambivalent about being a girl, choosing to mask herself as a boy in order to minimize challenges from adults, almost all of whom fall victim to the male patriarchy or enjoy exercising their power because of it. The ultimate "hysteric" in the novel is Liza Tillerman, Dicey's mother. Abigail, Dicey's grandmother, almost suffers the same fate and is regarded by some in her community as "mad." Cousin Eunice has, as one student stated:

> a shriveled soul, trapped by a joyless, hopeless routine and driven by her own neurotic obsessions and a relentless sense of duty that has actually turned her into a self-absorbed martyr.

Yet Voigt's casting of Dicey as the protagonist means hope in that man's world. Although she chooses subterfuge in her disguise as a boy, Dicey retains the female role of caretaker. Similarly, although Abigail is described as "mad" by her neighbors, she can clearly survive without men. The primary female characters in the novel are emotionally strong, intellectually and physically competent; they are farmers, sailors, and circus acrobats who have rejected the destructive influence of the males in their worlds.

I found Voigt's portrayal of Cousin Eunice particularly savage. Unlike Liza, for whom we can feel sympathy, or Abigail, for whom we can feel admiration, Eunice is portrayed as someone who has capitulated to the male-dominated hierarchy and is pathetic because of it. She defers to male authority figures such as Father Joseph in a way that suggests total subservience:

Father Joseph, Cousin Eunice's friend, was a priest, a slender, restless man with thick gray hair and deep lines in his forehead. He had cool, thoughtful, light-brown eyes, deep set, and a thin mouth. He wore shiny black trousers and jacket, a black-shirt front, and the band of white, crisp and stiff, around his neck. Cousin Eunice introduced him and *fluttered nervously around him on her high-heeled shoes, bringing him a cup of tea and offering him a tray with a little china pitcher of milk and a little china bowl of sugar cubes.* (p. 122; emphasis added)

One wonders why Voigt seems to have such little sympathy for Eunice. One also wonders why Eunice doesn't see what Voigt's narrator sees: the calculation suggested in the "cool" eyes and "thin" mouth, and the un-yielding aura in the white band "crisp and stiff around his neck." This image, juxtaposed with Eunice's "fluttering" around Father Joseph in her "high-heeled shoes," suggests that Eunice is aware of the power differ-ential but chooses to capitulate. As many of my male and female stu-dents argued, she, too, is a victim, but she has given up what neither Liza Tillerman nor Abigail gave up: her capacity to love. Liza Tillerman may have had to finally face defeat and admit to being unable to care for her children, but she releases them in good faith, to her nearest relative. Abigail, stated one of my students, "learns from Dicey that love does not have to mean submission." Eunice, on the other hand, seems to have "lost her emotional center," as another student stated. The children's first en-counter with Cousin Eunice presents a similarly unflattering portrait:

A short round woman wearing high-heeled shoes walked towards the steps where they sat. The little round woman . . . walked past again, from the opposite direction and on the opposite side of the street. . . . She was wear-ing a plain black cotton dress and had short gray hair that was permanented into sausage-like curls that bounced and jiggled on her round head. (pp. 116–117)

More telling is Eunice's apology to the children for initially walking past them:

"And then, of course, to see four children on my doorstep. Well, I had no idea. You don't mind, do you? You aren't offended? I was afraid. You hear of such strange things happening these days. . . . I hoped you would go away. If Mother were here of course. . . ." Her voice drifted off, her eyes drifted away from them and out to the windows. (p. 118)

She agrees to take the children because "How could a Christian do less" (p. 129). She doesn't talk so much as "sigh." She is weary. She is resigned in every aspect of her life. Her job as foreman in a lingerie factory, where she supervises attending lace insets to lingerie, is "a responsibility. You wouldn't believe some of the pieces of lace they expect us to set" (p. 136). She teaches classes in religious instruction, but these, too, are tiring. She is not *mad* in the sense that Dicey's mother is, but she can be read as the suppressed hysteric. We wonder with Dicey "what kind of work would make a person look like that" as Eunice curls "over onto the tabletop, her face pale and her eyes, lack[ing] expression" (p. 136).

And so we find ourselves repelled rather than impressed with her heroism when she decides that she will take care of the children, giving up her dream of becoming a nun because "that is my duty" (p. 151). Our suspicion that Cousin Eunice enjoys the role of the martyr is confirmed when she declares that she will relinquish her dream of becoming a nun in order to become a substitute parent for Dicey and her siblings. Like Dicey, I too, felt the urge "to get up and run" (p. 151).

So I come back to the question of why Voigt cast Eunice in such an unsympathic light. I am convinced that Cousin Eunice is a victim of the patriarchical system and is *mad within it*, as Dicey's mother is *mad outside it*. Both women, in essence, suffer the same fate—the destruction of their identities and the destruction of their essences. They have been leeched of self. One capitulates but seems sane, while the other capitulates and is declared insane.

The foregoing discussion of women as victims of the patriarchal system brings my discussion to a consideration of the social and cultural situatedness of both writing and reading. Many of my own struggles (and those of my students) with my responses to the characters and their actions is a reflection of our situatedness as readers. As one of my male students wrote:

> What I initially saw as a universal classifying system (that is, villain, hero, martyr) I now had to acknowledge was my own value system. It occurred to me that what I was doing was applying my own value system based on the behavior of the characters.

We might, as this student did, respond to the text because of our own "leftist leanings" or "feminist leanings," but Voigt's presentation of her characters and their situatedness within the social and cultural contexts they occupy are not without significance either.

Homecoming: A Socially and Culturally Situated Feminist Reading

In another piece of work (Soter, 1997) I suggest that understanding the meaning of others' responses requires that we understand our ideological stances inherent in cultural and historical cultural and historical influences on our ideological stances as readers. We should also consider the stance of the writer from this perspective.

My response, from a feminist perspective, reflects a change in my own awareness of reading patterns in texts that I formerly read with what Fetterley (1978) might call my "immasculated eyes" (p. xx). I cannot help but be aware that my current readings of the novel are a result of values that reflect greater awareness of the ideological and political nature of roles that have traditionally been assigned to men and women. Although assigned stereotypical roles, Eunice and Liza Tillerman are women for whom I *can* have sympathy, but sympathy will not be allowed to turn to empathy, for they are cast as social and cultural victims and not role models. Voigt appears to favor the strong women in this novel—Dicey, Abigail Tillerman, and Claire—who consistently defy the social and cultural constraints typically experienced by women. Dicey, for example, is not a classic beauty—she is rather flat-chested, skinny, dour, lank-haired, and intellectual. Abigail Tillerman is handsome rather than beautiful, rejects softness and maternalism, is completely self-sufficient on her farm, and is regarded as "queer . . . crazy as a coot" by the locals. Claire, although attractive in a stereotypical way (red cloud of hair, very tight jeans, and high heels), is a dog trainer at a circus. All of them hold their own, especially when confronting men who attempt to intimidate or subjugate them.

Throughout the novel, most of the women generally fare better than the men, who come across as either selfish, insensitive, authoritarian, intimidating, or irresponsible. These men are also frequently threatening in appearance, such as the security guard at the shopping center who calls to Dicey:

> "Hey kid," he said, as if she had shown signs of running and he needed to bait her. He was heavy, out of shape. He had a pig-person face, a coarse skin that sagged at the jowls, little blue eyes and pale eyebrows, and a fat, pushed-back nose. (p. 16)

A similarly threatening and unappealing image is drawn of Mr Rudyard, who hires the children as fruit pickers for a brief period:

> His face was square and blunt. . . . He moved toward the Tillermans without hesitating, without hurrying, and stood silent before them. . . . He reached his napkin up and wiped his mouth.
> "Yeah," he said. (p. 221)

With compelling consistency, we are given a negative view of men in terms of how they have affected the women in Dicey's life. As Dicey reflects on the events that led to their abandonment by their mother, we see that Voigt does not want to condemn the mother. The third-person narrative representation of her when the novel begins has a sympathetic cast:

> The woman put her sad moon-face in the window of the car. "You be good," she said. "You hear me? You little ones, mind what Dicey tells you. You hear?" (p. 1)

This sad but well-intentioned attempt at mothering is followed by the image of Liza Tillerman's "stride made uneven by broken sandal thongs, thin elbows showing through holes in the oversized sweater, her jeans faded and baggy" as she walks away from them (p. 9). Dicey's later recollection of the events that led to her mother's disappearance includes her mother's loss of her job; her mother's refusal to meet with Maybeth's teacher; her mother's aimlessness and blank-faced stare as she sat at the kitchen table; the silence; her strange, childlike behavior; and the realization of the possibility that her mother had "gone crazy" (p. 13). Voigt gives us all this information before we find out that the children's mother has truly gone away with no forwarding address. We are also given to believe that she had made some preparations for leaving them and that she truly loves her children (although we see this only through the children's eyes): "We already have a good mother! Dicey said angrily to herself," when Cousin Eunice suggests that if they stay with her, they will have a "good mother" (p. 152).

What signals does the text give us of how we should "read" Liza Tillerman's situation? Is it too much to suggest that the text guides us into viewing her sympathetically? That we are positioned by the text to view her as a woman with no education to permit advancement, with no male support, worn out with trying to bring up four children? The text gives us evidence, time and again, that she had simply become tired and could think of no other solution to the daily struggle than to give up. It is the stance of innocence as well as of victim and is reinforced by the children's and Abigail's recollections of her in better times, that in these times "She was gentle—like Maybeth" (p. 301).

The book also documents what happens when women marry. In response to Dicey's question "Why didn't Momma want to get married?" (p. 300), her grandmother reveals that "She had seen what happens. She didn't want to give her word, like I did. We keep our promises, we Tillermans. We keep them hard" (p. 301). She subsequently reveals that in her own 34-year marriage, she had been docile and submissive. After her husband died, Abigail tells Dicey, she found herself, hence her reluctance to be caught up again in family responsibilities:

> "Since he died, I've been different. It took a while but—it's my own life I'm
> living now. I had a hard time getting it. I don't want to give it up. No lies, no
> pretending, no standing back quiet when I want to fight." (pp. 300–301)

How much has been kept hidden as revealed in those words? Abigail's
view of marriage as a constraining force in which she is unable to be truthful to herself, to what she knows and feels, is further revealed in her admission that

> "I was angry—most of my life. . . . Not any more—if you can believe that.
> Just crazy now and that's an improvement. Not really crazy. Eccentric. But
> those years, morning to night. All that anger—you can choke swallowing
> back anger." (p. 302)

Finally, she releases the deepest truth, the consequences of her denial of
truth and of keeping her promise to love, honor, and obey her husband:

> "I failed them. I let them go. I told them to go. There were times when I
> could have killed him. He'd sit chewing and anger and shame were sitting at
> the table with us. Chew and swallow, so sure he was right. But I'd promised
> him—and he didn't know why they each left. I did. So I'm responsible. I
> won't have that responsibility again. Not to fail again." (p. 302)

One woman, then, rejects the system's suppression and exploitation of all
women. Whatever Voigt says about her intentions with this novel, it is
difficult to *avoid* a feminist reading of it.

APPLICATIONS OF FEMINIST CRITICISM
TO OTHER YOUNG ADULT NOVELS

An interesting comparison can be made between *Homecoming* and Colin
O'Brien's *Z for Zachariah* (1974). Both novels have female protagonists who
must make their own way in the world. Both novels also have males who
are presented in a threatening and dominating manner. O'Brien's novel,
however, also presents a female protagonist through male eyes and suc-
cessfully blurs the gender lines.

Katherine Paterson's *Jacob Have I Loved* (1980) offers interesting possibilities for a discussion of suppressed sexuality in Paterson's portrayal of
the sexually obsessed grandmother who attributes sexual motives as an
explanation for all the other characters' actions. The grandmother also
offers another view of the "hysteric" female figure discussed earlier in this
chapter and the conditions that cause such "madness" in some women.

Along the same lines, teachers could also compare and contrast similar female figures in novels such as Emily Brontë's *Wuthering Heights* (1847/1947) and Charlotte Brontë's *Jane Eyre* (1847/1960). Although not a "hysteric," Louise, the protagonist in *Jacob Have I Loved*, appears, like Dicey in *Homecoming*, to be androgynous in the early stages of the novel. She initially aspires to become a lobster fisherman rather than follow more traditional female career choices and later dreams of becoming a doctor. Ultimately, she trains as a midwife, which many of my female students term a "cop-out." The novel offers interesting possibilities for a feminist analysis in terms of the promise it seems to offer as a story about a strong-willed young woman who, in the end, capitulates to the partriarchal model of the ideal woman. My female students invariably resist the concluding section of the novel, which suggests that it carries more psychological truth than they might want to admit.

Turning attention to Paul Zindel's *The Pigman* (1968), we find a novel that provides us with a male and female version of the treatment of an old man through the lens of a male author. Nevertheless, it provides rich material for an analysis of male/female versions of reality, relationships with others, and, thus, a discussion of how reality is defined in gendered ways.

In essence, a feminist reading can be applied to any novel, whether written by a male or female author, if one asks the question: How do we read and write as men or women? Indeed, recent feminist criticism has become interested in comparative gender analysis—perhaps a natural outcome of at least one effect of feminist criticism in that feminism has functioned as a "force that disrupts the symbolic structures of Western thought" (Spivak, quoted in Culler, 1982, p. 49), suggesting that, although we are all, women and men, constructed by the collective unconscious, we have the potential to disrupt our prior conditioning.

QUESTIONS AND ACTIVITIES FOR FURTHER EXPLORATION

Questions

Questions that reflect a feminist orientation and which could serve as the basis for individual projects as well as classroom discussions include:

1. How does the novel show that women's assumed biological attributes are sources of strength rather than weakness (a position taken by some radical feminists)?
2. Does Voigt's novel illustrate that divisions among women might sustain the patriarchical system in which they live?

3. How does the novel show ways in which women "see life differently from men" (Selden & Widdowson, 1993, p. 211)?
4. How does the novel portray men and the effects they have on the women's lives in the novel (e.g., Father Joseph wants to control; Rudyard threatens, as does the security guard)?

Questions that focus on a gendered reading could include:

5. How do boys and girls perceive the males and females in both novels?
6. To what extent are these perceptions based on the experiences and beliefs students bring with them to their experience of reading the novels?
7. Do male students feel marginalized in reading *Homecoming*? In reading *Z for Zachariah*?
8. How do both genders respond to the presentation of strong, competent women in both novels?

Other questions could focus on a gendered view of the authors and how they wrote the novels:

9. How are males and females presented in the novels?
10. Are there male/female differences in the ways in which the authors resolved conflicts in the novels?
11. Are there differences in the ways in which the authors have presented the female protagonist that could be attributed to their own gender differences?
12. In what ways is the writing discernibly "male" or "female"? Among possible foci, students might consider features such as appeals to the emotions of readers, ways in which characters behave, and perceived challenges to gendered stereotypes.

Activities

1. Consistent with exploring this novel from a feminist perspective, a teacher might have students research Voigt's own life and the extent to which *Homecoming* reflects themes in that life. For example, we know that Voigt supported her first husband while he was in college. During that time she stopped writing, although she had been writing much during her college life (Garrett & McCue, 1989). Voigt says that her writing was in many ways a symptom of what was wrong in her marriage (Garrett & McCue, 1989). She left and supported herself and her daughter by washing floors and tutoring and began writing again. These early events suggest the sources of Abigail Tillerman's anger over living her life through her husband. There are also parallels with the women who are represented as abandoned in *Homecoming*.
2. Some students might read *Dicey's Song* (Voigt, 1982), the sequel to *Homecoming*, and explore patterns in the ways in which Voigt treats men and

women in both novels. They could then analyze such patterns in terms of how they reflect a "woman's" view of the world, relationships between men and women and among women, and women's aspirations and how they are or are not fulfilled.

3. Other students could explore how women are portrayed as marginalized in this novel and how the author presents women who do not fit social and cultural norms. For instance, the "madness" of the mother, the portrayal of Maybeth as "dumb" when much of her external behavior can be attributed to her fragility and vulnerability, and Dicey's boylike appearance and how that serves as well as undermines her.

A college teacher might also want students to explore to what extent feminist criticism permeates other critical perspectives. One way of doing this would be to ask students to identify features of the novel that reflect multiple critical perspectives; for example, genre criticism, psychological criticism, Marxist feminist criticism, and reader response criticism. They could then examine ways in which each perspective reflects a gendered reading and in doing so move to what Culler (1982) describes as the broader struggle of which feminism is a part, that is, the notion that feminist criticism is a political act—an attempt to change the way we read so that we might rewrite "feminist" criticism as "gender" criticism:

> [Gender] criticism is a political act whose aim is not simply to interpret the world but to change it by changing *the consciousness* of those who read and their relation to what they read. (Fetterley, 1978, p. viii; emphasis added)

CHAPTER 4

Looking at the Past Through the Present: A New Historicist Reading of My Brother Sam Is Dead

Historians can no longer claim that the study of the past is detached and objective. We can never transcend our own historical situation . . . the past is something we construct from already written texts of all kinds and which we construe with our particular historical concerns.

(Selden, 1989, p. 95)

RETHINKING RELATIONS BETWEEN HISTORY AND LITERATURE: NEW HISTORICISM AND CULTURAL CRITICISM

According to Louise Montrose (1992) "in the 1980s, literary studies in the American academy came to be centrally concerned with the historical, social and political conditions and consequences of literary production and interpretation. . . . The writing and reading of texts, as well as the processes by which they are circulated and categorized, analyzed and taught, came to be seen as 'historically determined'" (p. 392). In short, literary texts would be viewed as products of a time and place, much as any other form of discourse, whether written or not. Furthermore, literature would not be seen as more significant (or privileged) than other forms of discourse (James Phelan, in conversation, November 5, 1996).

As a consequence of this shift in perspective, the determination of meaning became problematized, according to New Historical Critics, by including an examination of the processes by which meaning and value are produced and grounded. Clearly, New Historicism has close ties with Marxist criticism and also shares boundaries with the more recent phenomenon known as cultural criticism or cultural studies. Common to these perspectives, however, are the following: (1) the view that history is anything but an orderly sequence of events; (2) the view that writing history means telling *a story about a story of past events* (rather than simply telling a story about past events, which presupposes our ability to do so objectively,

45

and representing that telling as a "true" account of those events); (3) the view, espoused by both Althusser (1976) and Foucault (1979/1988), that every aspect of our lives, our attitudes, and our beliefs is shaped by social institutions and ideological discourses. Foucault (1979/1988) also believed that that these discourses are "historically dominant ways of controlling and preserving social relations of exploitation" (quoted in Selden, 1989, p. 164). Simply put, no text is innocent: All texts are products of the time in which they are written as well as products of a history within a particular social, cultural, and ideological context.

According to Green and LeBihan (1996), Stephen Greenblatt's *Renaissance Self-Fashioning* (1980) marked a new kind of historical criticism that replaced the notion of history as continuous and coherent with the view that it is not unified, not continuous, and definitely not coherent. Influenced by Foucault, Greenblatt and other New Historicists also disrupted the traditional notion of literary text as separate from other discourse, with the result that boundaries between history and literature are blurred rather than clearly defined. Furthermore, since history came to be viewed as indeterminate and a matter of representation rather than "fact," historical writing cannot be considered as anything but a matter of interpretation. Therefore, if we perceive history and historical writing solely as acts of interpretation, they are as subject to indeterminacy, speculation, and partiality as any other form of discourse.

Although Traditional Historicist Critics saw literary history as part of the political, social, and cultural context that it inhabited (Selden, 1989), poststructuralists saw this context as marginalized in traditional Historical Criticism. That is, Traditional Historicist Critics accepted the political and sociocultural context as given fact—something that remained, in effect, *outside* the critique of the literature that represented the period in question. New Historicist Critics also believed that historian-critics are as influenced by their contexts as the texts that they critique and not unaffected by the values and attitudes of their own time—values and attitudes that color their critical analyses. Every act of expression is contextualized (Green & LeBihan, 1996).

If we accept this, authors, too, must be affected by the ideologies of the time in which they are writing, for according to Selden (1989), all human life is shaped by the institutions and the ideological views of its time. Thus, if we follow this reasoning, it is possible, for example, that an author may not even be aware that the content of his or her novel might suggest a critique of some event or of some beliefs pervasive during the period of writing that novel. The authors of *My Brother Sam Is Dead*, for instance, claim that the novel had no connection with the era during which it was published. New Historical Critics would argue that it could not help but reflect a critique of the Vietnam War, although its ostensible subject is the American Revolutionary War. The past, they believed, could no longer be viewed objectively (Selden, 1989), nor "can we transcend our own historical situation" (Selden, 1989, p. 163). Instead, we "construct" the past (Selden, 1989, p. 163), doing so in a way that reflects our own personal agendas and concerns.

Given that we buy into New Historicist notions of history and its writing, we could argue that the genre in which history is reconstructed is immaterial. Therefore, historical fiction is a legitimate literary form through which to represent an event in the past. Indeed, it may be an apt vehicle through which to present a revisionist view of that past event at a time when it might not be considered patriotic to do so. For example, a novel about a war in which the motives of both sides in another (but unstated) war are questioned, and in which questions about the nature and value of patriotism are explored, might escape censure more effectively than would a discursive exposition of these subjects. For despite what New Historicist Critics claim, I would argue that fiction contains a level of aesthetic ambiguity that often escapes definitive interpretation. On the other hand, the censuring of literary writers during the McCarthy era certainly suggests that one of the main tenets of New Historical Criticism withstands scrutiny: that is, that literary and nonliterary texts are indistinguishable, at least in terms of subject matter, if not form.

That is the perspective I found myself adopting following my second reading of My *Brother Sam Is Dead*. In a sense, then, we are deconstructing a reconstruction of the past—a past already interpreted by the authors who chose to represent it in their work.

JAMES L. AND CHRISTOPHER COLLIER'S
MY BROTHER SAM IS DEAD: A SYNOPSIS

The novel opens with a scene in which the protagonist's family and friends are debating the course of the fighting that has already erupted between Loyaltist (pro-British) and Rebel forces during the early onset of the Revolutionary War. Sam (the protagonist) bursts in on this scene and a subplot—the parallel conflict between Sam and his father, Life—is revealed.

Caught in the middle of the conflicts are 11-year-old Tim, the apparent narrator, and his mother, Susannah. Both are powerless to affect the course of events. Yet both are also the survivors—Sam and Life finding death through betrayal at the hands of the forces they each separately support.

As the conflict between the colonists and the British intensifies, so does the conflict between Sam and his father. Sam leaves Yale, where he was studying, to join the colonists against his father's wishes, and Tim, the narrator, finds himself in the uncomfortable position of mediator between the two. Through Tim, we learn news of Sam and the colonists' cause; through Tim, we also hear the voice of the authors, questioning the validity of war as a means of achieving independence, particularly when the war comes to Redding and begins to affect the lives of civilians. For the greater part of the war, Tim and his family are relatively unaffected, regardless of which side (Tory or Rebel) seems to be in the lead. However, reports of food shortages and scarcities in cloth, gunpowder, and leather mount as the war continues. But, as Tim reports, "most of the time, the war stayed away from us" (p. 86). The turning point comes when his father embarks on his annual journey to sell and trade cattle in Verplanks, New York, about 40 miles from Redding. Because of the war, neither Sam nor Tom Warrups (an occasional assistant) is available to go with him, so Tim accompanies Life on the journey.

Tim and his father are attacked by a group of Rebel cattle thieves on the journey to Verplanks, but during this first incident, they are saved by Loyalists, known as Committees of Safety, who chase off the thieves and help round up the scattered cattle. For most of the remainder of the journey to Verplanks, they are accompanied by an armed escort. With business completed, the return trip is uneventful until it begins to snow heavily and they are forced to take a more direct route back to Redding, the route on which they had been attacked. In the process, Tim and his father become separated and Tim discovers that his father had been ambushed by what he assumes were the same cattle thieves who had previously attacked them. With considerable ingenuity, Tim manages to convince the thieves that he is expecting an escort and manages to escape from them but is never able to find his father.

With his father and brother gone, Tim becomes the male head of the family, helping his mother run the tavern. As he observes of the changes that have happened, the "biggest one . . . was happening inside" himself (p. 132). He becomes aware that he is no longer a boy in the way he shoulders his share of responsibilities and, in particular, the way he begins planning what had to be done. For a short time he believes he is a Tory and not a Rebel—a result of his father's capture by the Rebels. That, too, changes dramatically when the British troops come to Redding, kill several innocent people, and set fire to the home of one of Tim's friends.

From this point, the drama escalates significantly, for the war has finally come to Redding. In the process, Tim and Sam meet again, and Tim discovers that in their relationship, too, there are significant changes. He sees that Sam's claims that he is a Rebel soldier for patriotic reasons is hollow and that Sam is really a soldier because he loves the excitement and the "thought that he is doing something important" (p. 163). By December 1778, hunger is widespread in the area, the Rebel forces seem to be making headway against the British, but morale and ethics have reached a low point among them. It is in this climate that Sam becomes a victim of his own cause. Because of the extensive cattle thieving by the Rebel troops —a result of the hard winter and the widespread hunger—the Rebel generals decide to execute some of their own as a warning to the rest. Sam is one of the intended examples. Tim is unable to save him, despite two attempts to plead with General Putnam and Colonel Parsons; and although he attempts to rescue Sam, he cannot prevent the execution. The story (although not the novel) ends with his graphic account of Sam's death.

The story is told retrospectively—a reconstruction from the memory of a now 64-year-old Tim, who takes us back to the beginning of Sam's involvement in the war effort on the side of the Rebel forces. Readers do not discover the disguised narrator until the epilogue, so they view the whole account through the eyes of an 11-year-old Tim.

A NEW HISTORICIST–CULTURAL READING
OF *MY BROTHER SAM IS DEAD*

In discussing this novel from the traditional textbound perspective, we might comment on the plot structure as reflecting conflicts between those for and against the Revolutionary War. Within this structure is the father–son conflict between Sam and his father, Life. A major thematic strand is that in war there are no winners, a message conveyed through Tim. Because he is on the fringe of the action, restricted because of his age from direct participation in the war, Tim is able to ask questions that an older person could not—to do so would be suggestive of simple-mindedness rather than simplicity (e.g., "Aren't the Rebels just as bad as the Loyalists?"). Many of the characters are flatly drawn, functioning primarily to further the action of the plot; not even the protagonist, Sam, can be perceived as "dynamic," that is, a character who undergoes transformation and growth in response to the events that occur. Even Tim, the narrator, is not given much psychological depth—a consequence of the authors' choosing to present the main action of the novel in the form of a flashback from the perspective of a much older Tim (64 years old), a grandfather, reflecting on what the cost of the war has been:

> Father said, "In war the dead pay the debts of the living," and they have paid us well. But somehow even *fifty years* later, I keep thinking that there might have been another way, beside war, to achieve the same end. (p. 211; emphasis added)

Revising History: The Past Through the Present

We do not discover this until the end of the novel. So, what invitations are given by the text to read it as something other than a story about *that* American Revolutionary war and about how a particular family deals with the divisions and conflicts that this war brought about? The novel does provides us with a variety of signals that suggest we might want to reconsider the above reading, giving credence to Roger Fowler's (1977) claims that the way we shape our language in text can have dramatic effects on our interpretation of that text. Fowler further argued that "Language abounds with constructions which express, or draw attention to the actions performed and required, the attitudes displayed and desired, by and in the participants in the act of communication. . . . These are explicit manipulatory structures" (p. 42).

The most salient clue is in the novel's revisionist stance on the war. The Colliers do not present it as a glorious chapter in American history. Rather, we are told that even the original motives for the war are suspect:

> "These agitators can always manage to stir up the passions of the people for a week or so, but it never lasts. A month later everybody's forgotten it— except the wives and children of the men who've managed to get themselves killed." (p. 7)

Although Life Meeker is a Loyalist, his reasons for arguing against war are personal, yet ideological:

> "Principle, Sam? You may know principle, Sam, but I know war. Have you ever seen a dear friend lying in the grass with the top of his skull off and his brains sliding out of them like wet oats?" (p. 21)

We find ourselves agreeing with this man. He is the voice of reason, of concern for what matters most to him: his family, his friends, and human life in general. In contrast, the Rebel cause, no matter how apparently justified, comes through as the ravings of a bunch of unprincipled hotheads. That the cause of reasoned human behavior is represented through Life Meeker is not an accident but a transparent signal that even war fought for freedom is not justifiable. It is also not an accident that the Rebel cause is argued largely through the actions and words of a naive, excitement-seeking 16-year-old:

> "So anyway, some men were killed. I don't know how many, and then the British went on up to someplace called Concord looking for the ammunition stored there, but they didn't find much and turned around and started

back to Boston. That was when the Minutemen really peppered them, they chased them all the way back home." (p. 5)

If the Colliers wanted us to see the war as valid for the sake of principle, would they not have chosen a more mature, seasoned voice through which to argue it? By choosing Sam to represent the case for the Revolutionary War, they cast doubt on the motives of those who pursued it.

true?
or is Tim
the
protag.?

In applying New Historical Criticism from the Marxist/cultural critical perspective to *My Brother Sam Is Dead*, we would ask, for example, what the most important cultural influences to be aware of are in both the writing and production (publishing) of this novel. We would ask ourselves what the Colliers had in mind by choosing to use a *child's* voice to carry the questions related to whether or not the Revolutionary War was justified, or why the child's voice is the medium through which the authors foreground questions concerning the motives and values reflected in either side (Loyalists and Rebels). We would also consider what is being signaled in revealing not only the traditionally perceived conflict between the British and the colonists but also the confrontation of the traditionally accepted view of the colonists as unified against the British. Finally, we would contextualize the book not so much in terms of the period it describes as *by whom it was written and when it was written*. The rewriting of history, in other words, brings about a re-viewing of the events presented in terms of the present rather than the past. In this sense, we would also find ourselves asking for what purpose(s) this particular novel was written, for which historical audience it was intended, and how should we use this knowledge (Foreman & Shumway, 1992)?

All these questions also move us to a consideration of authorial intention, to the notion that authors manipulate language, and to the idea that language is not innocent.

I realize that I am going to run headlong into potential debates about the validity of authorial intention, but I will pursue this path regardless because of the shaping of the language in this text (Fowler, 1977). That is, the Colliers have deliberately constructed their text in such a way that we question a war that has traditionally been held as a symbol of democracy and of the right of a people to determine their own destiny. The Colliers have hardly chosen an "innocent" structure: A 64-year-old man recounts the events of this war from the perspective of himself as an 11-year-old. The child's account cannot be free of the 64-year-old's knowledge, values, experience, and emotions. Why choose to tell the story from this perspective? Why not simply have the 11-year-old tell the story? What does such an account, told from the older man's recollective vision, give to the dimensions of the tale? Who is the reliable narrator here—Tim at

11 or Tim at 64 or neither? Does it even matter, since the authors have stacked the cards with what amounts to fairly blatant authorial intrusion, as we discover toward the end that we have, all along, been reading the *reconstruction* of these events from an older man?

One of the consequences of having a narrator who is actually mature is that there can be no growth, no development in the characters—something we have come to expect in young adult novels, no matter which genre. So we have to ask ourselves: If this tale is not about the development of particular characters as they respond to events and to others around them, what is it about?

What we are left with is to consider the purpose of the narrative structure, and this points directly to the purpose of the authors. Having an adult tell the story of the war, even if through the eyes of his reconstructed younger self, is clearly a signal that we are to read the novel as a commentary on that war. Further, this narrator could be accused of being selective in *what* he chooses to remember and *how* he remembers it. Additionally, we are not given any evidence that Tim had kept a diary or had access to any documents in his reconstruction of the war as he retells it. All we have to rely on is his memory. The title also prevents us from becoming too involved in the action—we know that the protagonist's brother is going to die. We are not able to invest ourselves in his fate. It seems that we are being directed to engage with the novel in an evaluative way, *to think* rather than to feel. This does not mean that we escape emotional involvement entirely. Life and Tim's encounter with the Rebel cattle thieves is a suspenseful incident in the novel, for example. Similarly, it is difficult, if not impossible, to avoid the shock of Sam's death, even though we have anticipated it throughout the entire novel. However, the authors are consistent in their emphasis on philosophical and ideological issues—they want us to engage in that debate and foreground it frequently throughout the novel.

As a result, we can see the novel as not so much about the American Revolutionary War as about all war. Furthermore, given the publication date of the novel, it is not a great leap to recontextualize the novel as a critique of the Vietnam War—a war that was generating fierce ideological debate in the United States at the time when the novel was being written. That is, we "reject the dichotomy between background and foreground" and, instead, perceive "literature as both reflecting and creating a certain cultural reality" (Phelan, 1994, p. 39). If we accept that the Colliers are themselves "written by the culture in which they wrote" (Phelan, 1994, p. 39), then we have to contextualize the novel as a product of the time in which it was written rather than as an imaginative product about an event in the past.

Even if we don't accept the novel as a revision of the Vietnam War rather than the American Revolutionary War, it does appear to reflect and re-create the cultural reality of the period in which the Vietnam War was fought. The protests against the Vietnam War were not only a reflection of a desire to not be involved in a war that was perceived to involve another country's issues. They were also a reflection of a general questionning of the reasons that have traditionally been given as a rationale for all wars: fredom from oppression. Once cherished ideals such as this are questioned, it is not surprising that we might question even the grounds upon which earlier, more sacred wars were fought. Thus, the Rebels in *My Brother Sam Is Dead* are *not* the heroic figures we might expect them to be.

A Problematized Reading

In an epilogue to the novel, the Colliers state that "in writing this book we have stuck to history as closely as we could," although "[we have] also made a good deal up" (p. 212). Many of the characters in the novel actually existed and "act as we believe they would have acted under the circumstances" (p. 214). The shooting of Sam Meeker was "taken as much as possible from the shooting of the real John Smith" [a 17-year-old soldier who, along with the butcher, Edward Jones, was executed by General Putnam "much as we have described the death of Sam Meeker" (p. 215)]. They claim they do not have an answer to the question the whole novel poses: "Could the United States have made its way without all that agony and killing?" (p. 215). If the Colliers' claims are to be accepted, why the revisionist representation of the American Revolutionary War? What did they seek to correct in condemning the Rebel cause as much as the Loyalist one? How do we read the juxtaposition of the following examples: the war-wearied Rebel generals and colonels; Tim's profiting from the war; the loss of life; questionable ethics by both parties; assertions by both parties that the war is fought for "liberty and justice for all"; the murder of a boy because the Rebel leader is a "great patriot"? Tim's questioning of the justifications both sides give for the war begins early:

> To be honest, I wasn't sure Sam was right about the fighting anyway. It sounded right when he said it—that we should be free and not have to take orders from people who were so far away, and all that. But I figured that there had to be more to it than Sam knew about. (p. 9)

As we follow Tim's reconstruction of the story of the war, we are regularly presented with evidence that the Rebels were not as pure in their cause as their ideological arguments suggest. Furthermore, although the

British troops do not escape censure (for example, when they arrest Tim's young friend, Jerry Sanford, and decapitate Samuel Smith's slave, Ned), the critique focuses on the Rebels' actions. We could read this as a critique not only of wars in general, therefore, but also of those classic justifications for patriotism. When one of the Rebel leaders, Captain Betts, asks Tim to ring the Redding church bell in order to alert his soldiers that they will pursue the British after they have captured Jerry Sanford, Tim's mother refuses. Astonished at her refusal, he demands, "Where's your patriotism, woman?" (p. 149). She replies:

> "Bah, patriotism. Your patriotism got my husband in prison and one of my children out there in the rain and muck shooting people and likely to be dead any minute, and my business half ruined. Go sell your patriotism elsewhere, I've had enough of it." (p. 149)

According to the Colliers, ends do *not* justify means. Readers will also see that Sam is unjustly convicted and that the ethics that determine his execution are questionable. For example, the Colliers have provided *contemporary* readers with this revealing admission from Colonel Reed:

> "Here's the problem. Those soldiers Sam caught with the cattle are scared to death Putman will decide to hang them all as an example. They're prepared to tell any kind of lie about Sam to get themselves off. . . . Then there's the fact that Sam comes from a Tory family. . . . [But] the board will do whatever they think General Putnam wants. And if they decide that Putnam wants to make an example of somebody, they'll hang—they'll bend over backwards to satisfy him, regardless of the evidence." (pp. 189–190)

The question of right and wrong is brushed aside in the interests of pragmatic decision making when those in authority cannot retreat from a decision they have already made because they fear that doing so would weaken their authority. The cattle and supply thieving by roving bands of colonists who capitalized on the chaos created by the war are simply presented as despicable—morality is not a privilege of the underdog. Ideals that fed the Revolution are cast aside and decisions are made on the basis of ends justifying means, as Tim discovers when he finally makes contact with Colonel Parsons in his quest to save Sam from execution:

> "Do you want to know what General Putnam is thinking? It's this. He's thinking that he can't win the war if he doesn't keep the people on his side. He's thinking he can't keep the people on his side if the troops are running amok among the civilian population. . . . So many men have died, so many mothers have wept, so many brothers and sisters have cried. He is thinking that in the long run if he executes somebody, he'll shorten the war and save more

lives. It doesn't matter to him very much who he executes; one man's agony is like another's, one mother's tears no wetter than anybody else's. And that's why he is going to have Sam shot." (p. 194)

It may seem far-fetched to consider *My Brother Sam Is Dead* as a political document—that is, as an opportunity for the authors to influence young readers through the way in which they depict the most sacred of U.S. wars, yet such a perspective is not out of the question if New Historicists are to be believed. Reenvisioning and revising history have become more popular with the notion that *how we view an event is what determines our understanding of it*. The Colliers' strategy of using an apparently neutral narrator, too young to be involved in the action, retelling the events from a now-adult perspective, enables the authors to offer authorial comment that seems to imply criticism of war and yet leaves open the possibility of considering war as a dilemma that does not yield easy answers:

> It will be, I am sure, a great history. Free of British domination, the nation has prospered and I along with it. Perhaps on some other anniversary of the United States somebody will read this and see what the cost has been. (p. 211)

The juxtaposition of images—one of greatness and prosperity and the other of the cost involved—prevents us from making a simplistic judgment of war. Tim struggles with this ambivalence, finally asserting that neither side was "right":

> So Father had forgiven Sam, and I think Mother did. . . . But for myself I wasn't sure. I knew I'd be glad to see him, and have him home; but still I felt it was partly his fault that Father had died . . . he was fighting on their side, and I couldn't easily forget about that. . . . It seemed to me that everybody was to blame, and I decided that I wasn't going to be on anybody's side any more; neither of them was right. (p. 167)

Some readers may be troubled by these examples of the ambivalence, but the Colliers' represent, I believe, the relativity typical of postmodern thought. That is, they and their work are products of the time in which they are written.

APPLICATIONS OF NEW HISTORICISM TO OTHER YOUNG ADULT NOVELS

It is possible that a novelist might adopt a New Historicist position in writing about a past war, especially one that has been surrounded by the halo of a battle fought for freedom. A critical reading of such a novel would then "uncover" such a position. At the same time, readers might adopt the same perspective relative to their reading of that text, thus, in effect, second-guessing the authors and the extent to which that which is stated reflects that which is not stated. Although I have argued that on one level *My Brother Sam Is Dead* reads as an anti-war document, it can also be read as reflecting ambivalence, although that may not have been the authors' intent.

As stated in the introduction to this chapter, in adopting a New Historicist perspective, particularly with a Marxist slant, we can also read fiction as reflective of the attitudes and values of the time in which it was *produced*. Widespread disillusion was pervasive in American society at the time of the writing of this novel. The values that enabled a nation to fight with a sense of unity during World War II and the various wars and potential wars of the Cold War era (e.g., the Korean War, the Cuban missile crisis, the early phases of the Vietnam War) were no longer as readily believed as they had been.

If one of the goals of a New Historicist reading is to uncover how "discourses are always rooted in social institutions" (Foucault, quoted in Selden, 1989, p. 96) and to examine how such discourses are "merely historical ways in which control and the preservation of social relations of exploitation are preserved" (Foucault, quoted in Selden, 1989, p. 96), then we could explore fiction functioning unwittingly as a servant in that cause. In other words, novels may seem to challenge the established order but, in effect, affirm it, as many young adult novels do. My students have argued that although many young adult novels appear to disrupt the status quo, the inclusion of "happy endings" or, at very least, endings that yield hopeful resolutions, undercut the disruption. More advanced students in the secondary classroom could explore that phenomenon in novels such as Hughes's *A High Wind in Jamaica* (1929); Avi's *Nothing But the Truth* (1991); Cormier's *The Chocolate War* (1974) and its sequel, *Beyond the Chocolate War* (1985) or Paterson's *Jacob Have I Loved* (1980). Each of these novels appears to convey a powerful challenge to established, cherished beliefs, and yet each leaves the reader wondering how far this challenge really goes. Various writers have suggested that in writing young adult fiction they are faced with a difficult predicament that those who write adult fiction do not have to face; that is, the difficulty of leaving young readers with no hope of resolution. And yet one could argue that this is also the predicament of an era in which we appear to have a desire to "tell it as it is" but have not yet found what we will put in place of our cherished but stripped illusions.

QUESTIONS AND ACTIVITIES FOR FURTHER EXPLORATION

Questions

If teachers choose to view this novel through the lens I've suggested, the following questions might provide a focus for starting a discussion:

1. Could this novel have been conceived of in the period following the War of Independence? When could it *not* have been published? Why not?
2. What was going on during the time of the writing of the novel—socially, politically, culturally? How could it be argued that the Colliers were products of their time in terms of the issues that play out in this novel?
3. Given that we accept the possibility that the novel is a product of a set of cultural and political views held during the 1970s, what has this to do with the way we think of the Colliers' choice of an 11-year-old narrator?
4. The authors claim to be representing fact through fiction. To what extent do we take them at face value?
5. What view of history is proposed? How is it presented?
6. Is the novel itself a "site for struggle"? If so, what is the nature of that struggle? Has the novel ever been censored or listed for censorship? By whom? For what stated reasons?
7. How could the position taken by Tim (and, by extension, his creators, the Colliers) be seen as a marginalized view of the war?
8. Are the authors the "I" as represented by Tim? What role does this narrator play, and who is the ideal narrative audience?
9. Why did the authors choose to represent their view of this historical event in the way they did—that is, in fictionalized form? What does their choice of genre and mode tell us?

Activities

To answer some of these questions, teachers might prompt their students to pursue several activities, including the following:

1. A biographical study of the authors in an attempt to connect the text with their own lives, attitudes, and other works in order to perceive whether there is a pattern in their work.
2. A study of other works by the Colliers—that is, a study across texts to determine the extent to which they use their fictional writing to "instruct" readers.
3. A study of the role of the narrator through Sam's, Life's, or Susannah's voice—all representing differing views about the war. What happens to our own views of war when we make these transpositions?

As students consider the above questions and concerns, teachers can turn the discussion to an exploration of the strengths and weaknesses of writing historical fiction as both history and good fiction (that is, a good story). Among some of the possible strategies, teachers could ask some students to write about an event in the form of historical fiction, while others could write factual accounts of that same event. Students might consider how their own perspective on war or some other subject leads them to prefer one subgenre over another, that is, choosing historical fiction in preference to a biography or a discursive essay on the same topic.

When students are asked to make decisions related to choice of genre and mode relative to their perspective, they will be able to better consider how choice of character, point of view, and perspective (positive, negative, or neutral) all play on the reader. These activities can then lead students back to a discussion of *My Brother Sam Is Dead* as both an effective piece of historical fiction and an effective piece of history.

- Rhetorical critic 檔 = discussion of narrative structures & rhetorical purposes.
  - how narrative techniques work on reader
  * concerned w/ whether an author's narrative strategies have achieved their intended result.

- Point of View:
  - 1st, 2nd, 3rd ...
- Reader/Text/Author Relationships
- 4 Kinds of Audiences constructed by authors:
  - actual audiences
  - authorial audiences
  - narrative audiences
  - ideal narrative audiences

} Hypothetical & reflect authorial intent regarding interpretation of text.

Overview: Ch.1 → 4 dimensions of perspectives: view relative to readers, view relative to context, view relative to text, & view relative to author. Our position as readers determines perspective. Different literary theories.

Ch.2 → Psychological: Tyler

Ch.3 → Feminist: Leigh

Ch.4 → New Historicist:

Ch.5 → Perspective/Narrator Strategies: Leigh

Ch.6 → Deconstruction:

Ch.7 → Cultural Response:

Ch.8 → Summing Up: Leigh

Chapter 5: Playing w/ Perspective: Narrator Strategies in Where the Lilies Bloom

CHAPTER 5

Playing with Perspective: Narrator Strategies in Where the Lilies Bloom

The act of joining the narrative audience or not, is not the ultimate step in literary interpretation . . . it is the first, essential step. And many novels fail to make an impact *because readers do not join in the narrative audience.*

(Rabinowitz, 1976, p. 133; emphasis added)

RHETORICAL APPROACHES TO READING

With its roots in Plato's and Aristotle's works, rhetorical criticism asks us to consider how readers, texts, and authors function in relation to each other. Although we cannot entirely exclude the contexts in which each of these are placed, the main interest of the rhetorical critic is a discussion of narrative structures and rhetorical purposes. The reader's role is defined in terms of how particular narrative techniques work on the reader—that is, the *effect* of certain narrative strategies on the reader (Selden, 1989). Although the reader retains a significant role in the interpretive process, rhetorical analysis focuses on *how* the author accomplishes those effects. Rhetorical criticism is, therefore, an evaluative criticism, concerned with whether an author's narrative strategies have achieved their intended result.

Within this broad interest in how a literary work plays on readers, the Chicago School (neo-Aristotelian criticism), through its most influential voice, Wayne Booth (1983), proposed that we also consider distinctions between authorial voice and narrative voice. In doing so, we attempt to tease out values and attitudes of authors from those of narrators, distinctions that have implications for whether authors chose the traditional narrative roles of first-, second-, or third-person point of view. For example, the choice of first-person narrative in young adult fiction may initially suggest that the first-person narrator is *not* the author's voice. The protagonist appears to be distinct and separate from the author (the mimetic illusion). However, an author may employ narrative strategies that dispel this illusion before too long and so reveal that all along, the protagonist has been speaking for the author as well as him- or herself. On the other hand, the Chicago School argues that "all narration is a construction behind which resides an implied author who cannot be identified with the narrator" (Selden, 1989, p. 31), but the extent to which this can be supported could be refuted by, for example, psychoanalytic criticism, which denies this separation between the writer and the literary work created.

In believing that all art is an "imitation of perceived reality" (Selden, 1989, p. 31), the Chicago School argued that literature is, in effect, an artifice that assumes authorial intention. Other rhetorical critics do not agree with Booth (e.g., Phelan, 1996) as to whether or not authorial intention is something we can actually recover, as Booth (1983) suggests. More important, however, rhetorical critics such as Phelan (1996) take Booth's concepts of the rhetorical function of narrators and contexualize them in reader-based critical theories. Phelan's (1996) interest, in particular, is in the relationships among authorial agency, textual elements, and reader response and the ways in which each of these influences and can be influenced by the others. Thus, although Phelan (1996) remains concerned, as do all rhetorical critics, with the effect of a literary work on the reader, his rendering of it complicates interpretation and, he argues, "enriches our readings of texts" (Phelan, 1996, p. 19) because he takes into account not only the text and how *it* affects readers but also what *readers and authors* bring to their transaction with that text. In this sense, Phelan and critics like Crane (1953) depart from traditional rhetorical criticism because they do not perceive textual elements (that is, the "art" or "craft" of the literary work) as separate from the contexts they occupy, whether these are the world being imitated or the actual world in which the text as well as readers and writers are always situated.

The idea of contexts and constructs is also related to another central concept in rhetorical criticism; that is, Booth's (1983), notion of reliable and unreliable narrators. According to Booth (1983), in fiction, as soon as we "encounter an 'I,' we are conscious of an experiencing mind whose views of the experience come between us and the event" (p. 152). Implicit in this is the suggestion that the reliable narrator is someone we can trust and, therefore, is close to the author, perhaps even the author in disguise. On the other hand, the unreliable narrator is, as Booth (1983) says, "mistaken or believes himself to have qualities which the author denies him" (p. 159). In judging a character who functions as a narrator (the dramatized narrator), the reader will join with the author in judging that character as reliable or unreliable. This, in turn, affects the reader's perception of not only the narrator but also other characters and the work as a whole. If the narrator is unreliable, readers must be able to respond in such a way that they do not lose empathy for the narrator (usually the protagonist) while, at the same time, they receive reliable information from elsewhere or in another way. Authors who use unreliable narrators often, though not always, employ irony as a rhetorical device in order to accomplish this goal, so that readers indirectly receive the information they need to make sense of the events and perceive them as intended by the author, if not the narrator.

[handwritten margin note: vehicle for propaganda]

Connected to any discussion of reliable and unreliable narrators are their rhetorical equivalents, the authorial and narrative audience (Rabinowitz, 1976). Both of these are implicitly authorial constructions, and both are dependent on the effectiveness of authors in constructing their preferred audiences as much as on the willingness of readers to enter the rhetorical triangle (writer, text, reader). Rabinowitz (1976) suggests that there are at least four kinds of audiences that authors construct: actual audiences, authorial audiences, narrative audiences, and ideal narrative audiences. Actual audiences are, in effect, real readers, and although authors seek to influence them, the extent to which they do so is dependent as much on readers as it is on authors and the strategies they employ. Authorial, narrative, and ideal narrative audiences are hypothetical audiences and reflect attempts by authors to position readers relative to how close or distant they want them to be to the characters and events in the literary text.

According to Rabinowitz (1976), we must become members of the authorial audience in order to bridge the distance from our initial location in the actual audience and enter the world constructed by the author. Once we have entered that world (that is, become the authorial audience) and have temporarily left our own behind, we either find ourselves completely suspending our disbelief and, in effect, merging with the characters and so becoming the narrative audience, or we position ourselves as the audience the author wishes he or she were writing for (the ideal narrative audience). In the case of the ideal narrative audience, we accept uncritically what the author has to say.

These distinctions may seem unnecessarily fine until we consider why readers find novels convincing or unconvincing. For example, if we fail to enter the narrative audience, we cannot take that vital first step of suspending our disbelief, which subsequently enables us to accept any of the constructed world that the author has created for us. An example of this inability to enter the narrative audience (whether or not it is ideal) is when younger readers expect a story to match their perception of actual reality. Thus, an unsophisticated reader would reject the notion that a protagonist, who might be an unreliable narrator, does not see and know what we see and know. They would not be able to make the distinction that in the novel, we have entered a constructed world in which reality (as we perceive it) must, to some extent, become shaped to fit the world of the text. At times, too, readers may simply resist the author's invitation to enter the narrative world—perhaps an indication that the initial signals by the author failed to achieve their intended effect. Alternatively, the inability to move from actual to narrative audience may stem from a misreading of the rhetorical cues provided by the author, a consequence of not understanding relationships between literary form and content.

Finally, it is worth noting that rhetorical criticism enables us to consider literary works from multiple perspectives. As we consider narrators and their roles in texts, as well as our roles as audiences, we are also simultaneously able to view the text through a variety of other lenses, for example, feminist, deconstructive, psychoanalytic, and so on. We are able to do so because the primary interest in rhetorical criticism is in the relationships among reader, text, and author and, within this broad set of relationships, how writers create texts that affect readers in various ways. That is, given our interest in understanding the *effects* of various narrative strategies a writer might use, we could view those effects by reading against them in a feminist and deconstructive reading or by reading through them in a psychoanalytic reading.

VERA AND BILL CLEAVER'S *WHERE THE LILIES BLOOM*: A SYNPOSIS

The novel is set in the Appalachian Mountains of western North Carolina, where the Cleavers themselves had established a home. Mary Call, the protagonist, takes us into her wildcrafting world and, early in the narrative, introduces us to her family, for whom she is, effectively, both father and mother. At 14, Mary Call is not the oldest child, but she describes herself in ways that initially, at least, leave us in no doubt as to her competence to be head of the family. Devola, her 18-year-old sister is, according to Mary Call, "cloudy headed" (p. 3) and not regarded as having enough wit to care for them all. At the time we first meet the children, Roy Luther, their father, is seriously ill and their mother has been dead for several years.

We follow Mary Call's efforts to care for her brother, Romey, and her two sisters, Devola and Ima Dean, by gathering herbs (wildcrafting) and selling them to the local general store and drug company. Her concern about money is compounded by a debt her father owes to Kiser Pease, a local wealthy farmer. Mary Call's perception of Kiser as a mean, greedy, and ugly person is not shared by Devola, whom Kiser wants to marry— an event that Mary Call is determined to prevent. She is also determined to find a way to have Kiser relinquish his hold on their land and home, and that opportunity arrives when Kiser develops a mysterious illness. With the help of her siblings, Mary Call cures him but, while he is still weak, extracts his signature from him, believing she has succeeded in having the land released to her family. It is when Roy Luther dies that she decides to make wildcrafting a full-time occupation. Meanwhile, they believe that they must hide Roy Luther's body until they can bury it, fearing discovery by their neighbors and county authorities. Through a series of minor disasters, including a bitterly cold and snowy winter and her own illness, Mary Call is unable to prevent Kiser and Devola from marrying. However, as shared guardian of the younger Luthers, Kiser proves to be a generous provider, helping them repair the battered house and building a barn for the livestock. He also formalizes the transfer of the land and house to Devola and her family. The novel ends on an optimistic note, with the return of spring and Mary Call's plans for expanding her business as a wildcrafter.

It is a novel about growth, a rite of passage, during which Mary Call learns that she is not always right, that she must share her burdens with others, and that they are as reliable and competent as she is.

NARRATIVE POINT OF VIEW AS A RHETORICAL STRATEGY IN *WHERE THE LILIES BLOOM*

The Cleavers could have ended this novel when Mary Call receives a visit from Kiser Pease after he has "got the business of Roy Luther [i.e., his death] straightened out" (p. 206) and she thanks him for it:

> "You're welcome," said Kiser and grinned wide and I saw then his newly repaired teeth, shining white and clean and perfect.
> It would have been wrong to take notice of them in words so I didn't. (p. 206)

It is in this shift of perspective, this change of regard for Kiser Pease, that Mary Call's "journey" in this novel comes to an end. What a different view of Kiser from the one given us by Mary Call when we first meet him early in the novel:

> Kiser whimpered suddenly and pulled at the blankets. His eyelids drooped and two skimpy tears rolled down. He can't even cry generous, I thought, and leaned forward to feel the heat coming from him. His breath and the sight of his stained teeth, with dark brown pockets along the gum lines, recoiled me. (p. 23)

Narrators as Rhetorical Cues

Because we already trust Mary Call, we have no reason to doubt her view of Kiser at this early stage in the novel. In fact, there is not yet the slightest suspicion that she is untrustworthy (or unreliable) as a narrator. Yet, over the course of the novel, the Cleavers subtly reveal that Mary Call's view of others is not always accurate. As a result, we, too, find ourselves beginning to revise (as she does) our view of them and of her.

The choice of narrator can tell us much about an author's position relative to his or her characters. Booth (1983) claims that "if an author wants to earn the reader's confusion, then unreliable narration may help him" (p. 378). Why would the Cleavers want their readers confused? What effect did they want to achieve by having their readers gradually perceive the protagonist/narrator appear to be unreliable? One answer to these questions is that the Cleavers have chosen misperception and ignorance stemming from overconfidence as the flaw for an otherwise remarkably competent protagonist. Once it is established that Mary Call is wrong and stubborn in her perception of others, we begin to wonder about her perception of Devola as well.

Many of my students have been unable to believe that a 14-year-old girl would not notice that her older sister is actually *not* "cloudy headed." They also found it difficult to accept that such a young girl could be competent enough to take care of her family as well as Mary Call tells us she is able to. It's not until we considered the implications of casting Mary Call as the narrator as well as a major actor in the events that my students began to accept the "realism" of this novel. Their initial reading suggests what Rabinowitz (1987) describes as a *"misreading"* (p. 42; emphasis added); that is, a reading based on *not observing* the narrative conventions in this text.

If we read, as Rabinowitz (1987) suggests, trying "to duplicate the angle of the author's attention" (p. 51), then we should pay attention to how the narrative is constructed, not just to what is being written about. In this case, we would have to ask what is being brought to our attention by telling this story from the perspective of a teenager who has seen little of the outside world and who has had limited access to knowledge from other sources. Questions that naturally flow from this include: What will she notice? What insights is she capable of? What are her strengths and limitations? Our reading usually begins with the title of the book and flows to the end. We develop our first impression of this teenager from her encounter with a stranger to her mountain hamlet during which Mary Call appears as a very assured young woman. We have, at this juncture, no reason to doubt what she declares:

> I said, "Don't pay her [Devola] no mind. She's cloudy-headed. Why did you say you had been to Sugar Boy and Old Joshua for the memory? That wasn't a real answer, was it?" (p. 2)

This casts a negative light on Devola's response, which had preceded Mary Call's:

> Devola thought this a funny answer. She laughed and ran down into the yard and hid herself behind a flowering rhododendron and peered out at us through its white, lacy veil. (p. 2)

Mary Call doesn't laugh and run away to hide behind flowers. She asks direct questions, she tells the stranger what happens in their valley with the assuredness of a seasoned tour guide. She appears an equal to this stranger as she affirms his declaration that "This is fair land; the fairest I have ever seen" with her reflection that "I have never forgotten what he said—that this land was fair land, the fairest of them all. This is where the lilies bloom" (pp. 2–3).

In paying attention to these seemingly innocent details, one is drawn to the *rhetorical* cues that Rabinowitz (1987) claims authors provide us with; that is, to rules of notice, rules of signification, rules of configuration, and rules of coherence (Rabinowitz, 1987). Briefly, rules of notice relate to what details of the text the author prioritizes (e.g., the first sentence and the last sentence of a paragraph). Rules of signification refer to those rules that tell us how to draw significance from what the author established in the rules of notice. Rabinowitz (1987) defines rules of configuration as referring to how the literature is organized in "clumps" (p. 44), such as plot patterns and formulas. Rules of coherence are about how a text makes sense, how it helps us deal with "inconsistencies," or whether the author has developed some "over-arching theme" as a means of creating unity in the text (Rabinowitz, 1987, p. 45). With this novel, it means we pay particular attention to *who is telling the story*. Unless we pay attention to the role of the narrator in *Where the Lilies Bloom*, we will most likely miss that which will enable us to *make sense of* (or resolve) what appear to be inconsistencies in the tale as relayed by its narrator.

Troubling Responses to *Where the Lilies Bloom*

As stated earlier, many of my students found the novel a problem because they saw Mary Call as an implausible character and an unreliable narrator. They have argued that she is too controlling, too pragmatic, too efficient, too competent, and too knowledgeable "for her age." They have believed that her solutions for Kiser's illness, her sagacity in keeping Roy Luther alive, and her finding a way of keeping his death a secret from the entire community until she secures her little family's land are too far-fetched for a typical 14-year-old (Soter, 1996).

Her comments often reflect the wisdom of an adult who has seen more of the world than the mountain village she inhabits. Is it really so unrealistic to assume that a child could be as competent as Mary Call, given her circumstances? Is it really so implausible that she could be as "grown-up" as she is in the ways of the world and in her sage understanding of the motives of others?

Answers to these questions can be found if we think of the novel as an accurate representation of a way of life that actually exists, a way of life that is quite different from what many of us might be used to. Although some of my students have experienced difficulties in their own lives, none have ever struggled with basic existence as Mary Call and her family must do. The Cleavers personally experienced life with the people of the region. Their images of the mountain people of Appalachia as "proud and independent" (p. 213) are in striking contrast with the more familiar stereotypical images of them as "ignorant," "crazy," "feeble-minded," and "waiting for the charity check" (p. 89). As the authors note in an epilogue to the novel, they were particularly impressed with the "friendliness and the simplicity and the friendliness of the people [who] envy no-one" (p. 213). One difficulty readers face in this novel, however, is that they must take a leap of faith (that is, enter the ideal narrative audience who know what the author knows) that the authors are indeed representing life as it is lived in the region described. If one excludes knowledge that the authors lived in the region for many years and based the novel on their experiences there, the opening chapters offer no clues that suggest we should believe, as fact, what is described about the region and its people.

Having explored thus far, I would like to examine one particular aspect of the novel that relates to its structure and point of view. According to several of my students, the evolution of events in the novel is poorly constructed. Devola's becoming sensible and capable after having been presented as someone who appears to be mentally retarded seems thoroughly implausible. How could she turn into the competent character she later becomes? Is this presentation a structural problem? Or is it an outcome of having chosen a narrator (Mary Call) who can *only* tell the story from the perspective of her own limited vision? Booth's (1983) description of reliable and unreliable narrators provides a clue here:

> It is most often a matter of what James calls inconscience; the narrator is mistaken, or believes himself to have qualities which the author denies him.

... Although (as in Huck Finn) the narrator may claim to be wicked while the author silently praises his virtues behind his back. (p. 159)

If we consider the following excerpts as evidence of the *power* of the first-person narrator in creating authenticity, the problem is no longer a structural one but, rather, a clever solution that enables the authors to show how their main character grows in maturity over the course of the novel. As Mary Call becomes ill and less able to handle her responsibilities, she begins to see what she had formerly not seen—namely, that her sister, Devola, is not retarded; that Kiser is well intentioned; and that her attempt to keep the family together without the help of others is futile.

First, we have her own statements about her competence:

It's because I'm tough . . . I'm so tough that if a bear came out of the side of the mountain over there I could knock him cold without even breathing hard. And that's all and if anybody's got a better idea how I should handle this and all the other things left to me just let them come on and tell me about it but I don't hear anybody saying anything. (n.p.)

We also know from her that she is practical and so believe more readily that what she says about Devola and others is an accurate representation of the facts:

Like I say, Devola is cloudy headed and this is one thing I cannot understand because none of the rest of us Luthers is that way but Devola is for sure, so each day I have to explain the whole of our existence to her. Her confidence in my ability to do this is supreme though there are four whole year's difference between her age of eighteen and mine of fourteen. (p. 3)

In contrast to Devola, Mary Call talks bluntly, matter-of-factly, a manner of speech we usually connect with people who are down-to-earth, no-nonsense, trustworthy:

Because he's ignorant. Nobody but an ignorant person would have a witch's keyhole in his house. And he's a greedy old gut and a cheat. There isn't another man in the whole world would come in here and sharecrop for him the way Roy Luther has for so little. Just years and years of it and when the time comes for tallying up, Kiser's always getting the hog's share and Roy Luther always having to settle for the meanest. (p. 7)

Given that the narrative is expressed in the first person, the authors must make Mary Call become so engrossed in her task of keeping the family together, retaining the farm, and keeping Roy Luther's death a secret from the valley that her attention to others, including Devola, is minimal. The authors must find a way of making Mary Call *notice* that she had it all wrong, and so she becomes ill. Someone has to take Mary Call's place as head of the family, and the only person who can do that is her older sister. However, before that can happen, the Cleavers must have us see Devola as competent, even though Mary Call cannot know how that competence developed. Only when Mary Call is presented with the evidence of Devola's competence as *fait accompli* can we see what she finally sees: "Luther never realized how much there is to her and I, myself, am guilty of this too" (p. 178).

Using the first-person perspective presented some major challenges for the authors. In the interests of realism, they had to be consistent. It is not *we* who see Devola, but Mary Call; and until she is able to see Devola as she truly is, neither can we:

> A sound coming from the front yard attracted us to the windows. . . . Devola was out there driving Kiser's car around, driving it around and around in a wide, easy circle. . . . "Well, for corn's sake," I said. And we went outside and stepped over the fallen fence and Romey lifted his hand, signaling to Devola to stop and she made one more graceful circle and brought the car around and came to a smooth stop in front of us. She leaned out and smiled and tenderly said, "See? I can drive. Didn't I tell you I could?" (p. 104)

The first-person account creates an illusion of truth that often trips the unwary reader, particularly if the narrator appears strong, independent, and resourceful—in other words, a person we can rely on. Our deliberations about whether we can trust the report we are being given are colored by our former decision about whether the narrator is or is not reliable when we first meet that narrator.

The limitations I referred to when an author uses a first-person narrator are not so much flaws as challenges that have to be resolved acceptably for readers to be able, in this case, to believe the transformation that Devola undergoes. Thus, although Mary Call *is* capable of reflection, it is not through her private reflections that we see her realization that Devola is not as she had perceived her to be—*rather, events are taking place elsewhere, and Mary Call has to hear about them rather than be involved in them* to be able to have the distance from Devola that is needed for her to be able to truly see her. Thus, Mary Call spends more time in the mountains at her wildcrafting and becomes more preoccupied with how she will keep Roy Luther's death a secret. Devola is learning to drive at Kiser's, to cook and keep house.

Nevertheless, while the authors must reveal that the narrator is mistaken, they must somehow have readers maintain a high regard for her because she is, after all, the protagonist with whom we have developed empathy and in whom we wish to believe.

Booth (1983) further observes that "observers and narrator-agents . . . can either be privileged or not, to know what could not be learned by strictly natural means or limited to realistic vision and inference" (p. 159). In this case, the Cleavers must perform a narrative feat by having Mary Call tell us about the actions of other characters in such a way that we also learn that they are not what Mary Call has perceived them to be and, simultaneously, having her appear to be ignorant of this revelation. Only in this way can the Cleavers bring us to see her own awakening later in the novel. This is accomplished through another recognizable device—as noted earlier, Mary Call has to become very ill and to suffer a fever. That narrative sleight of hand accomplishes two consequences: Devola must take over as the eldest and, thereby, demonstrate how competent and mature and sensible she has been (all the time), and Mary Call is, as it were, purged by the fever of her former illusions.

As we see through Mary Call's illusions, we join the Cleavers' authorial audience (Rabinowitz, 1976), that is, we see Mary Call as the authors have always seen her: as bright, perceptive, and competent, but also in need of growth and maturing insight. Apparent inconsistencies do become resolved with this reading of the novel. By considering the rhetorical techniques the authors have employed in their use of a first-person unreliable narrator, we become aware that we have only seen Devola through Mary Call's restricted vision.

APPLICATIONS OF RHETORICAL CRITICISM
TO OTHER YOUNG ADULT NOVELS

Many educators who have written about young adult realistic fiction (e.g., Donelson & Nilsen [1995]; Monseau & Salvner [1992]) have noted that young adult writers often favor the use of the first-person narrator. Many young adult authors do this well, enabling us to sustain our illusion that the story *is* being told by a teenager and not, in reality, by an adult. However, when using first-person narration, those authors are challenged to create an authentic perception on the readers' part. We have to believe that a 14-year-old, for example, really thinks, acts, and feels in the way presented. Such authors have to avoid suggestions of an adult consciousness guiding the narration to enable us to believe in the character. A second challenge is how to bring about change in a protagonist and how to record that change when self-report is the medium.

Paterson accomplishes a remarkable feat in resolving that problem in *Jacob Have I Loved* (1980) when she has the story function on three levels but uses the same narrator. The story begins with the adult Louise returning to Rass Island to take her mother back with her to Virginia. We are quickly moved into the past, to 13-year-old Louise, as if it were the present. It concludes with the return of an older Louise—but not yet the still-older Louise who is actually telling the story—to the mountains of Virginia.

Few of my students read the unmarked opening chapter in which Louise describes Rass Island. They quickly discern that it is mainly descriptive and, therefore, move on to the first chapter. In doing so, they miss vital information—in this case, that the story is being told by a much older Louise, who has been away from Rass Island for some time. Having this information means that we read the rest of the novel as a reconstruction of the past, a past filled with old wounds that, on being revisited, are bound to be painful when reopened. If we begin our reading with Chapter 1, we are already in the past with 13-year-old Louise and, if we maintain our illusion well, as equally ignorant as Louise about what the future holds.

Zindel's *The Pigman* (1968) provides a useful example of multiple first-person perspectives that resolve the problem of how readers see other characters through the eyes of an unreliable narrator. Both of the main characters (John Conlan and Lorraine Jensen) is a protagonist in this novel, each giving his or her own account of the death of Mr. Angelo Pignati. In Cormier's *I Am the Cheese* (1977), the use of first-person narrative is an excellent strategy for keeping us in the protagonist's mind, with the result that we ultimately do not know whether or not he was ever sure about where he was, about the past, or about the people and events he describes. Two historical fiction novels, Sonia Levitin's *The Return* (1987) and Hunt's *No Promises in the Wind* (1970), present opportunities for exploring the use of first-person narration with a genre in which authors are obliged to be historically accurate while presenting the fictional aspect of the tale through the voice of a young protagonist who would not be expected to have a sophisticated grasp of the issues of the chosen period. Some authors, as we have seen, choose to resolve this problem by having their protagonists tell their story retrospectively (see, for example, Chapter 4 of this volume for my discussion of the Colliers' novel, *My Brother Sam Is Dead* [1974]), thus enabling them to present information that an adolescent would not normally know. The peculiar challenge in first-person narration, however, is how to resolve the problem of using a narrator who is him- or herself confused (Booth, 1983), confusing the reader as a result, and how to convincingly bring about what Booth (1983) termed "demystification" (p. 284). The novels discussed above provide interesting and challenging examples of how authors achieve this to a greater or lesser extent.

QUESTIONS AND ACTIVITIES FOR FURTHER EXPLORATION

Despite, or perhaps because of, the troubling aspects of the use of an unreliable narrator, *Where the Lilies Bloom* nevertheless presents many opportunities for exploring narrator roles and the effective deployment of narrative strategy by the authors.

Questions

Questions that might be asked of this book (and other similar novels) include the following, which focus on the issues of reliable/unreliable narrators:

1. Is the narrator too self-interested to be "reliable"?
2. Is the narrator sufficiently knowledgeable to be "reliable"?
3. Is the narrator sufficiently "moral" to be "reliable"?
4. Is the narrator too immature to be "reliable"?
5. Are the narrator's actions consistent or too inconsistent with her words to make her "reliable"?
6. Who is doing the telling? Do you believe her? When do you believe her and when not? How do the authors imply that Mary Call's perceptions are vulnerable to self-deception?

Activities

Other questions might focus on the perceived effect of the authors' choice of characters and the development of events. These might be pursued through a variety of activities such as the following:

1. Students could write a letter to the authors about their perceptions of the characters, and then relate those perceptions to authorial intention.
2. Students could discuss several passages in the novel, selected by either the teacher or themselves, in terms of *what* these passages tell us about the characters involved.
3. Using the same passages, students could discuss how we are influenced by authors to attribute particular characteristics to their characters.
4. Teachers could have students rewrite the opening pages of the novel from different perspectives and discuss the impact that rewriting has on how they perceive the events. For example, the pre-chapter in which Mary Call tells us of her meeting with the stranger, who subsequently disappears from the book, could be rewritten from the stranger's perspective. Alternatively, the opening pages could be rewritten from the perspective of an absent narrator who proceeds to tell us about other family mem-

bers as well as introducing us to Mary Call. Questions arising from these could include: How do we perceive Mary Call's sister, Devola, in that rewritten perspective? How might that rewriting affect the later developments in the novel as told by the absent narrator in contrast to the narration being conducted by Mary Call?

5. Teachers could ask students to explore the opening passages of several other novels as well as *Where the Lilies Bloom* to compare and contrast the effects of choosing first-person narration with third-person narration and ask students to discuss what perceptions they receive of the protagonist and other characters as a result. These questions could lead to discussions of strengths and limitations of both types of narrative strategy as they influence our perceptions of characters and events. Some novels that would provide useful comparisons and contrasts include Avi's *Nothing but the Truth* (1991) and *The True Confessions of Charlotte Doyle* (1990), Voigt's *Homecoming* (1981), Paterson's *Jacob Have I Loved* (1980), and Paulsen's *The Island* (1988).

CHAPTER 6

Interpretational Play: Deconstructing
The True Confessions of Charlotte Doyle

I believe . . . that one can profit from a deconstructive critic's sensitivity to certain aspects of the play *of language.*

(Abrams, 1989, p. 336; emphasis added)

[handwritten margin notes: play / decon. not / about / play, but / secrets locked / in our / unconscious?]

DECONSTRUCTING DECONSTRUCTION: A BRIEF EXAMINATION OF THE THEORY

Deconstruction has drawn its share of criticism in recent years as a mode of critical inquiry that leaves the reader no closer to an answer about the meaning of a text than when the reader first encountered it. The never-ending circle of ambiguity that deconstructive criticism invites through its basic premise that meaning is forever indeterminate can, potentially, leave us even more confused than when we first began our inquiry from this perspective. And no matter how intensive the inquiry, it cannot assert what makes for the magical alchemy that results from the reading of some literary texts and not others. Further, with its intensive inward gaze, forever peeling off the layers of meaning (within and without the text), it also potentially carries its seeds of destruction, as its critics must not only deconstruct the text but also their own deconstruction of it. Nevertheless, Abrams (1989) sees that deconstructive critics have encouraged us all to see texts afresh, despite his caveat that such critics also "already know what [they] are going to find" (p. 330). As Abrams so succinctly describes it, a deconstructivist critic (e.g., Derrida),

> is an equilibrist who maintains a precarious poise on a tightrope between subverting and denying, between constructing and destroying, between understanding communicative "effects" and dissolving the foundations on which the effects rely, between deploying interpretive norms and disclaiming their power to "master" a text, between decisively rejecting wrong readings and declaring the impossibility of a right reading, between meticulously construing a text as determinate and disseminating the text into a scatter of undecidabilities. (p. 329)

Much has been written about the theory and practice of deconstruction since its primary exponent, Derrida, first described the concept and its implications for critical analysis. My purpose in this very brief account of what I perceive to be its most essential tenets is to provide the basis for a deconstructive reading of Avi's novel *The True Confessions of Charlotte Doyle* (1990). This necessarily highly reduced account may suggest that the theory is simpler than it has been described by its proponents, but that is not my intent. If readers wish to pursue the theory and its practice further, Green and LeBihan's (1996) Critical theory and practice, and Culler's (1982) *On Deconstruction* provide useful and quite insightful commentaries.

A useful way of thinking about Derrida's seminal notion of "difference" (the linchpin of deconstructive theory and practice) is found in Green and LeBihan (1996). "Difference" is not the binary opposite of "same." The concept, however, allows us to consider meaning as "uncovered" beyond what it appears to be on the surface of linguistic expression. Further, as we have "uncovered" what seems to be beneath the surface linguistic expression, we find ourselves "uncovering" that which has been "uncovered." That is, meaning is, indeed, indeterminate. As Derrida (1982) has argued, "difference" (or uncovered meaning, as I interpret it) is not *the* answer but "simply one more 'false entry' into the game" (p. 27).

Central to understanding deconstruction is the notion that "we are all colluders in the construction of meaning" (Green & Lebihan, 1996, p. 218). Essentially, we are all (writers and readers) perceived as engaged in the construction of meaning, and so meaning becomes dependent on *who* is engaged in that construction and *when* and *how* that construction is being carried out. In effect, our constructions are always contextualized in terms of who we are and all the circumstances that surround us at the time of those constructions—hence, the essential indeterminacy of meaning. In layman's terms, we could even argue that we are all involved in the process of deconstruction in our daily lives when we second-guess what someone says, thinking to ourselves that what is uttered is potentially the opposite of what is buried beneath the utterance. Another instance of how we often practice deconstructive thinking without perhaps being conscious of it occurs in the tension we experience in reading poetry when caught between literal and figurative language (Green & LeBihan, 1996, p. 221). Does the rhetorical question really signify a rhetorical question meant to be read as an ironic comment on what has gone before (i.e., as a statement), or do we take it at its literal meaning, as a genuine question, signaled, as it is grammatically, by the question form? Young and even older yet inexperienced readers typically do not understand that inversion of meaning implied in the rhetorical question because they are still focused on the form of the utterance and often, therefore, take such a question literally. Even the experienced literary reader may be taking a leap of faith in reading such an expression as a statement rather than a question. So we are brought again to the concept of the indeterminacy of meaning and, with it, the inevitable and potentially exciting view of language as the *play* of meaning. *who is playing? author or reader?*

AVI'S *THE TRUE CONFESSIONS* OF CHARLOTTE DOYLE: A SYNOPSIS

We first meet Charlotte, who is 13, on June 16, 1832. She is on the docks in Liverpool, England, searching for the *Seahawk*, a merchant ship owned by her father, who has arranged for her return to the United States with two families as her companions. In a very short time, she discovers that, because of illness, these families will not be traveling with her after all and she must continue alone and unchaperoned, the only female among a crew of merchant sailors. Although she is convinced her father would not approve and would delay her departure, Mr. Grummage, a business associate of her father's, will not hear of her remaining behind when the *Seahawk* sails.

Most of the rest of the action occurs aboard the *Seahawk*. Her initial meetings with the sailors do not bode well—she is warned that she should not be on the ship, they do not know what to do with her trunks, and she is linked with Captain Jaggery, who, she discovers, is feared and despised by all the sailors. The precariousness of her position on the ship becomes even clearer when one of the older sailors, Zachariah, befriends her and offers her a knife for protection. Before she falls asleep on this first day, a long and disturbing one, she overhears the captain and second mate, Keetch, discussing her presence on the ship as a trump card, a witness should the sailors dare mutiny. Before long, she learns from Zachariah that only the first mate, Hollybrass, is new to the ship; all the others had been on previous voyages with Captain Jaggery and had only signed up on this journey in order to seek revenge for his notorious cruelties. Trapped on the ship, Charlotte struggles with her natural loyalties to the captain, who takes care to treat her well and politely, and to her newfound friend Zachariah, whom she has no reason to disbelieve, although his story is fantastic. At first, her status as the daughter of the shipowner ties her to Jaggery, and so it is not surprising that Charlotte shows Jaggery the dagger given her by Zachariah. However, her emerging loyalties to the ship's crew win out and, at the last minute, she lies, saying the dagger came from Mr. Grummage, her father's business associate, who thought it might make her feel more secure. Charlotte also learns that Jaggery suspects a mutiny and requests that she inform him if she learns anything of it.

The journey is relatively uneventful, and Charlotte is slowly and guardedly accepted by the sailors because of her interest in what they are doing. While the ship is becalmed, she stumbles across a group of the sailors planning the mutiny. Although warned by them not to tell the captain, Charlotte feels she must. However, during the sequel of events, in which Jaggery shoots the leader of the mutiny and proceeds to whip Zachariah, Charlotte, unable to bear more cruelty, seizes the whip from Jaggery and lashes him across the face. She has lost what she thought was her protection, for the captain now abandons her. The crew also no longer trust her and refuse to hear her pleading that she was in ignorance and did only what she believed to be right. Only when Charlotte dons seaman's clothing and presents herself to Mr. Fisk, one of the mutineers who escaped detection, is she accepted by the sailors. Their acceptance also marks a radical change in her personality as well as her appearance, and it ultimately brings about the captain's downfall before the journey's end. When the ship docks in Providence, Rhode Island, both Charlotte's inner and outer transformations—from spoiled, wealthy teenager to resilient, toughened seafarer—are complete. The rough surroundings and unaccustomed crudeness of shiplife bring to the surface inner characteristics that had almost languished under the influence of her bland, unflurried, polished existence as the daughter of a man accustomed to exercising power over others. Throughout the journey, Charlotte learns to climb the ship's riggings, confronts the captain, joins a mutiny, is held captive, is almost executed, and survives it all. On her return, she finds she can no longer act as the submissive daughter of a father who will not hear "the truth" of what happened on her journey. When he burns the first account she wrote about her experiences and refuses to hear what really happened, she realizes she cannot return to her old life. The novel ends with her resolve to run away—back to sea and back to Zachariah, with whom she will presumably have many more adventures.

NARRATIVE PERSPECTIVE AND STRUCTURE: PLUNGED INTO A DECONSTRUCTIVE READING

Although *Confessions* might not be regarded as a classic *Bildungsroman* in the sense that Goethe's *The Sorrows of Young Werther*, Dickens's *David Copperfield*, or Brontë's *Jane Eyre* are, it nevertheless can be read as a "formation novel" (a literal translation of *Bildungsroman*) in that it is basically an account of how a youthful heroine undergoes a process of maturing, achieved through the various challenges she faces on a journey from Liverpool, England, to the United States. As discussed in Chapter 2, a key

highlights
reflect?
reflections

Since dumbed
down, prob use
in class

Personal Cannon —
gives a few ideas,
good activity?
DID NOT HELP CHOOSE BOOKS

Questions for class:
— title : believe/disbelieve
— oppositional pairs truth/lies
   what if we reversed them? hard/ea
— how does this disrupt our desire for unity?
— believe or not?
— Avi's intentions

read title

who's taken Lit Crit?
who's read Charlotte Doyle?

Lit Crit - deconstruction = post-struct. analysis of hidden
meanings in language
- get away from textual approach that accepts
it as a whole, story of growing up
- misleading that it's decon, but title is appropriate
* summarize Doyle book

Soter - look at discrepancies   journal, how get us?
- we construct the meaning - teach to students
- do we take it at face value? lady protests too
much "true" - Soter = literary hoax
- focus on reliability of narrator in retrospect,
written as if recorded currently but actually a
person (age?) recording past
- how we want to believe her

criterion for the "growth novel" is that it must be focused on this growth over time and situation, and there must be significant psychological insight on the part of the hero/heroine, not only about her own growth but also her perception of others, of reality, and of her role in the situations encountered. This psychological growth may then serve as a model for others, reflecting the early educational focus of this genre (the "upbringing" novel, popular in the late 18th century, especially in Germany). In initially defining this novel as a *Bildungsroman*, I am setting the stage for its subsequent "unveiling" in a deconstructive reading. Other categorizations (Donelson & Nilsen, 1995) have described it as a romantic quest story and an adventure story.

As in other *Bildungsromane*, the narrative seems to be innocently presented in the first person, but unlike them, the author, Avi, frames the account with a preface by the character, who warns the reader that she had been charged with murder, tried, and found guilty. She lets us know that she is taking us back to the Charlotte Doyle "she was" and that "although I have kept the name, I am not—for reasons you will soon discover—*the same* Charlotte Doyle" (p. 1; emphasis added). She informs us then that there are certain facts we should know before commencing the narrative proper—that this narrative is based on a journal her father required her to keep on her journey and that this journal is what enables her to "relate now in perfect detail everything that transpired during that fateful voyage across the Atlantic Ocean in the summer of 1832" (p. 3).

This framing is of interest—the rest of the novel is a retrospective account, although we do not know until the end just how retrospective it is. In the prologue we are *told* that the account is entirely based on Charlotte's journal and we accept this at face value, plunging into the narrative with Charlotte as she lived it. The surprise comes in the final chapter in which Charlotte relates the events that follow her return to her parents. At this point, we discover that her father burned her journal "to ash" (p. 221) and condemned it as nothing but "rubbish of the worst taste. Stuff for penny dreadfuls. Beneath contempt!" (p. 222): He chose to see it as the result of her teachers in England "filling her mind with the most unfortunate capacity to invent the most outlandish, not to say, unnatural tales" (p. 222). In light of this conclusion, the initial framing seems to function as a way for Charlotte to make her case and to *assert* her reliability as a narrator, for in the final chapter, we realize that as soon as she is able, she begins secretly to reconstruct her journal, to "fix all the details in my mind forever" (p. 223).

What we have in fact read is a *reconstruction of a reconstruction* of events and thoughts about them while Charlotte was en route (her journal, like most of its kind, being a retrospective account). This raises negative implications for our perception of Charlotte as a reliable narrator—for memory, as we know, casts an altered light on events. To add to this factor, memory that is now driven by anger and defiance may result in a rendering of the account in a way that casts Charlotte in a more favorable light. At any rate, the story is no longer a first-hand, freshly experienced account of events as they purportedly happened. To what extent the final narrative is a "fiction" of her imagination or, at best, an embellished account is left to *our* imaginations. We simply have no way of knowing whether to believe her father, who is, as she reports him, "an ardent believer in regularity and order" (p. 2), a man who seems stern, narrow, and rigid (e.g., his obsession with grammar and spelling rather than content). Yet he may also be a father who could be seen as any adult might be through the eyes of a crossed teenager and therefore might be, in reality, reasonable, responsible, and interested only in his daughter's safety. All the reports we have of her father are filtered through the *reconstruction* of the initial account, fueled by her defiant decision to do justice to her experience.

Nevertheless, long before we reach the final surprising revelation, we have been given an accumulation of evidence that Charlotte is capable of perceiving herself in a realistic manner, a factor that suggests her account is trustworthy. Thus, until we reach the point at which Charlotte reveals that the journal we are reading is not a first-hand account of the events, we see her as a reliable narrator. We accept her perception of the other characters, for we also hear her doubts, her motives, and her increasing understanding *as if it were happening* rather than as a narrative written after the fact. The internal view (Fowler, 1977) opens us to her states of mind, reactions, motives, and desires in a way that would otherwise be hidden from us. The risk that we might not believe what she says about Captain Jaggery, her father and mother, Zachariah, and the other ship-hands does not emerge until we consider the implications of the revelation that the events we are hearing about are reconstructions based on her original journal.

I have spent some time discussing the implications of the narrative perspective in this novel because it has a bearing on the extent to which we believe this rather extraordinary tale: how a sheltered, upper-middle-class girl survives her adventure as the only female on board a merchant ship whose crew signed on only in order to seek revenge against Captain Jaggery (as a result of cruelty endured on earlier voyages); how she not only survives such a trip but changes so dramatically to become a very adept deck-hand, shedding her elegant exterior self as well as her arrogant inner self; how she accepts the friendship and mentoring of Zachariah, an East African who, though never a slave, had run away from home; how she is able, in the face of her own scheduled hanging for allegedly killing the first mate, Hollybrass, to convince the remainder of the crew of her innocence and plan to reveal the captain as Hollybrass's murderer; how, even as she hangs by her fingers from a rope dangling over the waves, she tries to save the captain, who at that time is intent on shooting her to be rid of her testimony; and finally how, on regaining the safety of the deck, she assumes charge of the ship in response to Zachariah's words that "Miss Doyle here has done what we could not do. Let her be captain now" (p. 209). Even in the final decade of the 20th century, her feats are remarkable: She is more than Jaggery's "nothing but an unnatural girl trying to act like a man" (p. 206)—she has done what the men on the ship "could not do" (p. 206). As we have heard her tell the tale, we have come to believe all the extraordinary events because we believe have seen *inside* her—we believe we have seen all her doubts, her anxieties, her honest appraisal about returning to a world in which she will feel "pinched and confined" (p. 213), as she does physically when she dons her girl's clothes.

So Charlotte comes home to Providence only to find that her fond thoughts of how her family will receive her "in rapt, adoring attention, astonished yet proud" (p. 193) are an illusion. Instead, she is met with the "careful embrace of both my parents" (p. 214), and "even my brother, Albert and my sister, Evelina offered little more than sigh-like kisses that barely breathed upon my face" (p. 214). No words about her safety or her inner state, relief that she is alive and seemingly intact, come from her family. Her siblings comment on her clothing, her mother on how her face is "so very brown" (p. 214). Finally, her father asks if the voyage was "difficult" upon having noticed that the ship was "dismasted" (p. 215). As she begins to explain what happened, stating only that there "was a terrible storm . . . one of the worst they'd ever experienced" and that "we lost the captain" and "the first mate" (p. 215), her father simply responds that "one must be careful about the words we choose" (p. 215) and that "I look forward to a more sober account in your journal" (p. 215).

With this reception, we are more than ready for Charlotte to do what was most likely unthinkable for a girl of her time and of her class: She runs away back to the ship and sails off into the sunset with Zachariah, a "wind" which "has a mind of [her] own" (p. 226).

The growth that we expect to find in a *Bildungsroman* is satisfied on many levels, interior as well as exterior. The Charlotte we met as she first walks up the gangplank is gone. And yet we cannot be sure *who the real Charlotte is*. This uncertainty is set up by the novel itself primarily through the author's strategy of having her story told retrospectively and, presumably, edited as it must be by herself. Was Charlotte perhaps always given to invention? Is the story really a "fiction" as implied by her father? If so, why does Charlotte reveal his reaction to the reader? Had she wanted us to believe her without question, her father's view could be seen as damaging. And yet she presents her father as a controlling, highly conventional man who wishes to reassert his control over her. Who are we more likely to believe as a result of her own presentation? Initially, at least, most readers (including me) fall for her story. Her father's view of Charlotte can be perceived by the reader to be more condemning of him than of Charlotte. But can we really be sure that there is not a grain of truth in his assertion that she embellished the events. In response to her brief account of the death of Captain Jaggery and the first mate, he says: "It's well-known that sailors have a tendency toward exaggeration" (p. 215).

Charlotte constructs her case for the reader before her father calls her to discuss the journal by creating a contrast between how she now perceives the servants and how her father treats them. She lets us know that she sees them as equals, and the fact that neither servant can accept this—indeed they become nervous about her behavior—brings the reader onside when she writes in response to Bridget's "but it's my master who pays my wages" (p. 219):

> I looked into her eyes. Bridget looked down. I felt a pain gather about my heart. (p. 219)

On one level of interpretation, nothing appears amiss. Charlotte has taken us through stormy seas, murders, and mutinies with her. Why should we disbelieve her portrayal of her father? And again, why not? We could continue with this conundrum, but that is not the point of the reading. Rather, the novel repeatedly reveals opportunities for second-guessing, for *deconstructing* what is presented as one level of meaning with another. It provides us with a wonderful example of the ultimate ambiguity of language in literary play that, for me, began with a reconsideration of the structure and, later, the title of the novel.

WHY A DECONSTRUCTIVE READING OF *THE TRUE CONFESSIONS OF CHARLOTTE DOYLE?*

Steven Lynn's (1990) claim that "if structuralism shows how the conventions of a text work, deconstruction aims to show how they fail" (p. 106) provoked me to consider the possibility that deconstruction might not only show how textual conventions fail but reveal *how* an author has deliberately manipulated standard conventions *in order to* have them fail—that is, in order to be read in such a way that the reader *perceives* an intent that this text is not what it seems to be on the surface. Of course, irony has always had such an effect, and the reader who failed to perceive that the text was meant to be ironic has always been considered to have failed in the act of interpretation. However, with respect to Avi and, in particular, to this novel, irony does not initially appear to function as a rhetorical framework, and so I found myself turning to other possibilities, among them the notion that Avi might actually be playing games with us—perhaps for the sheer heck of it.

The serious goals of teaching literature in schools often preclude opportunities for what I'd like to term *interpretational play*. One of Grossman's (1990) graduate preservice English teacher's description of his approach to teaching poetry reflects what is very commonly practiced:

> I may talk a little bit about the title, and how the title relates to the poem, of course, but how that helps it—what the poem would be like without the title. And the choice of specific words such as "hunched"—why does he say "hunched"? Why does he say "fell"? And I would want them to see the parallel between dream and nightmare . . . the word "belly," why the word "belly"? (p. 90)

At this early stage in the student's teaching experience, the unquestioned assumption that this is how one "teaches" poetry is understandable, although troubling. As Probst (1990) points out, however, "knowledge of [literary] texts" is "traditionally, where most emphasis in literature instruction has fallen" (p. 106). That, in itself, is not a serious concern, but the narrowness of what constitutes "knowledge of text" is of concern. Implicit in the common practices of textual explication in schools is the notion that what texts and textual analysis provide is some kind of inherent truth about language and what is to be valued in language. Probst (1990) also argues that we need to teach students how to read literature critically so that they know how "texts suggest values and beliefs, how they push us, subtly or obviously, to accept the writer's assumptions and ideas" (p. 107). But should we not also *teach students the critical game—* that is, how to read *interpretation* critically and understand *how* we look at texts, how we interpret them, and how values and beliefs push us, subtly or obviously, to accept "critical assumptions and ideas" (Probst, 1990, p. 7)?

[margin note: Lit Crit for Kids]

One way of doing this (although I am sure there are others) is to *play* with criticism through *playing* with a literary text. Obviously, as in other cases I've described in this book, some literary texts lend themselves to this kind of analysis more readily than others. I found *The True Confessions of Charlotte Doyle* an ideal text both for this purpose and as a way to illustrate the notion of interpretational play. I have even suspected that the book might be an accomplished literary hoax—and a fascinating one at that.

[handwritten note: few contradictions w/ specific words, but many in reality—if you can get that far]

APPLICATIONS OF DECONSTRUCTION
TO OTHER YOUNG ADULT NOVELS

A deconstructive reading can be applied to any text, literary or otherwise. However, as with any critical perspective, we might ask what we want to accomplish with such a reading. Some novels, such as the one discussed in this chapter, will instinctively invite such a reading. Others will not, although a deconstructive reading might produce some surprising insights about both the text and our initial interpretations of it (see Abrams, 1989, for an interesting discussion of the appeal of deconstructive readings).

It may also happen that applying a deconstructive reading will result in further readings from other critical perspectives, such as feminism or cultural criticism, as we discover that closer investigation reveals the privileging of certain values or attitudes over others or marginalizes what we had not noticed in a prior reading. One might not even conduct a deconstructive analysis so much as adopt a deconstructivist *stance* toward language and its play, and this is what occurred to me during several readings of Voigt's *Homecoming* (1981), which resulted in subsequent rereadings from a feminist perspective. Another novel that may yield some interesting surprises, therefore, is Carter's *The Education of Little Tree* (1985), a seemingly innocent and authentic account of "a Cherokee boyhood of the 1930s . . . a felicitous remembrance of a unique education" (jacket copy of the University of New Mexico Press 1986 edition). The novel, originally published in 1976 and widely reviewed with acclaim, has since come under fire for its insidious disguise of the author's affiliations with the Ku Klux Klan. Something (structural, rhetorical, linguistic) in these novels triggers the suspicions of the reader that all is not what it seems to be, and, thus, a deconstructive reading appears to offer an interesting and worthwhile way of uncovering the layers of the text in an attempt to discover what has triggered that perception.

QUESTIONS AND ACTIVITIES FOR FURTHER EXPLORATION

A deconstructive reading naturally engages us in discovering the "rules of notice" (Rabinowitz, 1987, p. 43) that we have been unconsciously responding to in a literary text. What follows is a detailed listing of activities related to how we can use the text's signals in such a way that we read against them. Unlike in previous chapters, the questions and activities in this chapter are more detailed because they reflect the deconstructive process: one question uncovers another question in quick succession.

Questions

As teachers and students work their way through one question, others that are not given here will emerge. According to Selden (1989), Derrida resisted the notion of a deconstructive method. A "truly deconstructive" reading would, therefore, bring into question any truths uncovered in applying the deconstructive practice (Selden, 1989, p. 89). Consequently, the following questions should be reviewed only as starting points in the deconstructive process.

1. How does the title of the novel force us to engage in an act of complicity with the author in believing that the story which follows is to be accepted as presented by Charlotte?
2. What oppositional pairs might be found in this novel and in what order might they appear (e.g., truth/lies; fiction/nonfiction; land/sea; girl/boy)? What happens when we reverse the hierarchical arrangement in which they appear? What happens when we reverse what appears to be privileged by the author?
3. In what ways might this novel disrupt our desire for unity in a text?
4. How can we construct a case for believing Charlotte's account of the events in the novel? In what ways could that case be refuted?
5. Is is possible that Avi never intended for us to believe Charlotte's story?

Activities

1. Teachers might encourage students to identify which aspects of *The True Confessions* present them with signals that effectively ask them to "pay attention," even if they do not know why.
2. When students have been given an opportunity to record these impressions, they might share them in the whole-class setting. When I have done this with my own students, they are always surprised with the high degree of unanimity of these signals, including the title, the transformation of Charlotte, the burning of the journal, Charlotte's secret departure from her home, and the rewriting of the journal.
3. Students could then provide each other with reasons for identifying these elements. In order to confirm their intuitive identifications or Rabinowitz's (1987) "rules of notice" (p. 43), students might then return to a discussion of which linguistic and rhetorical *signals* alerted them to assigning significance to those signals. From there, they might be asked to consider the signals in terms of *patterns* (Rabinowitz, 1987, p. 44) that they perceive as related to them. At one level, this creates some discomfort as students realize that what they thought the signals implied about the outcomes—in this case, that Charlotte has provided us with a plausible

account of her adventures—often become signals to something else—that is, perhaps her story is all an invention. As students struggle to argue for or against this, they find themselves confronting "rules of coherence" (Rabonowitz, 1987, p. 45), that is, determining how the various parts of the work fit together as a unified whole.

4. Another activity that could be productive for a subsequent deconstructive analysis would focus on various constructions of Charlotte's character. Students could be divided into several groups, each group responsible for a particular view of Charlotte according to the following individuals: Charlotte herself, Captain Jaggery and her father, Zachariah, and their own reading of her. This activity forces students to confront the character as a construction, not only by the character herself but also by both author and readers. As students compare and contrast these views of the character, discussions inevitably turn to the grounds on which these perceptions are based, which, in turn, leads students back to the text for evidence to support or refute them.

5. A further possibility for a deconstructivist reading can be done through a comparison of students' perceptions of Charlotte's character with those of another in a novel narrated by either an absent or present "other." Paulsen's *The Island* (1988) is useful for this purpose. Wil's story is told through three perspectives (an absent narrator, Wil's journals, and Wil's diary entries). The result of such a comparison is to bring about a discussion of how narrative point of view affects not only our perceptions of characters and what they tell us but also how it affects our perception of "truth" in the telling.

6. The whole class could be engaged in a dramatization that is an extension of the novel: an imagined trial in which Charlotte must defend herself against the charge of fabricating the story as a cover for the mutiny of the sailors. Charlotte is still not implicated directly in the events leading to and from the mutiny, but she is an integral figure in the case. There is no evidence available, since her father burned the journal and Charlotte must be able to convince the jury that her reconstructed account is truthful. Students would use the text as their basis for interrogation, for Charlotte's testimony, and for final statements by both prosecutors and defense lawyers as well as jury deliberations. Involved in this exploration would be discussions of how language can be used to camouflage truth as much as reveal it. Also involved would be discussions of what is *not said* as well as what is said.

I would recommend a deconstructivist reading only with skilled readers who have already developed their own sense of the instability of texts and of possible ambiguities in meaning. The challenge of an endless and complex process of unraveling meaning as it can be presented through this novel is a fairly daunting task with younger readers, who are still struggling to make sense of the whole process of reading, a process that includes an understanding of such concepts as "rules of notice, signification, con-figuration and rules of coherence" (Rabinowitz, 1987, pp. 43–45). These are sophisticated concepts that experienced readers often take for granted even as they read for pleasure. When they have not as yet been estab-lished in the reading behaviors of novice readers, the uncertainties of a deconstructivist reading may present them with nothing short of a maze from which there is no escape.

CHAPTER 7

Reading Other Worlds: Culturally Situated Responses to Somewhere in the Darkness and Requiem

Readers' cultural practices of identifying with a certain character reflect cultural attitudes and values of certain groups. Understanding how students respond as members of a certain gender, or class . . . may serve to explain their responses.

(Beach, 1991, p. 126)

Readers resist texts and readings, as well as real and implied authors, because of their cultural memberships and various identity positions: as female, as African-American, as homosexual, as white students who resist challenges to their own privilege, or as Americans who cannot grasp the cultural meanings and values in stories of other countries. These communities, then, become sites of struggle (Eagleton, 1983) that we must navigate with a deeper understanding of culture and of difference . . . and the consequences of our cultural interpretive practices.

(Rogers & Soter, 1997, p. 4)

FROM THE OUTSIDE IN: READERS AND CULTURES

In many seminars and workshops, teachers interested in using literature of other cultures (whether ethnic or global) often remark to me that they do not know enough about the cultures represented in those books and are therefore hesitant to introduce such literature into their classrooms. Yet when the emphasis in literature instruction was on the text itself, many of us did not question the validity (or value) of teaching, for example, Chekhov's plays, Jane Austen's novels, or *Beowulf,* without knowing very much about the culture of the time and place in which these works were situated. However, we can no longer totally ignore the role of the cultural situatedness of authors, texts, and readers. Literary theory has driven us to recognize this phenomenon in the ways we talk about texts as well as in what kinds of texts are increasingly included in our curricula. The literary canon has expanded to include texts that challenge our sense of connection to them in overt ways through unfamiliar beliefs, values, social and cultural practices, and, sometimes, unfamiliar settings. What we used to accept as a truism of all "great literature" can no longer be generally assumed; that is, that no matter how different characters appear to be from what we know and believe, certain universals in human behavior will override those differences.

To a certain extent, some of us might still believe in those universals and argue that we have overemphasized difference in what have become known as "the culture wars" (Rogers & Soter, 1997) in an effort to bring recognition to groups that have long been marginalized. However, the inclusion of literature from outside the canon has highlighted issues that have always been present to a greater or lesser extent in the classroom: What is missed in reading literature of other cultures when we occupy the position of outsiders? Can we really fully engage with such literature? What kind of knowledge is needed to do so? What attitudes must we bring to the reading of ethnic and global literature? Is our resistance to such literature different from the resistance we might have toward literature representative of our own cultures? Are we really insiders of much of the literature supposedly representing our own cultures? What ideological forces are at work in how we should read literature of other cultures? There are no easy answers to any of these questions, but because we now have access to literary theories that address the roles of authors, readers, and contexts, as well as texts, we are in a better position than in the past to understand the interaction of all these in the process of interpreting and engaging in the literary experience.

Culturally situated response (Rogers & Soter, 1997), derived as it is from both reader response theories and cultural criticism, seems a useful frame with which to explore the above questions. The term acknowledges the presence and role of readers but also contextualizes them—that is, readers obviously bring individual values, attitudes, and histories to their reading, but they do so framed by the cultures they are part of, as are authors and texts. A brief discussion of those aspects of both reader response and cultural criticism that are relevant to my later application of culturally situated response to two young adult novels now follows.

Readers' Responses Within Cultural Contexts

According to Tompkins (1980), reader response is a "progression" evolving from a "variety of theoretical orientations . . . including new criticism, structuralism, phenomenology, psychoanalysis and deconstruction" (p. ix). In this sense, reader response theory embodies a variety of other critical perspectives that have always appeared to have been text-based. In essence, Tompkins sees readers as a common factor in the other critical perspectives she identified and as having an integral role to play in the literary transaction. As literary theory began to accept the notion that texts, readers, and writers are "inescapably part of the cultural contexts that create and recreate them" (Leitch, 1992, p. 163), critics' perception of readers have similarly broadened to consider how those contexts affect the ways in which readers perceive texts. This, essentially, is what cultural response means. Readers as isolated identities, subject to *internal* histories (as early response theorists such as Bleich [1978], Iser [1989], and Holland [1975] saw them), are gone; with the coalescence of many formerly isolated critical theories into what has become known as cultural criticism, our interests in any discussion of literature, its construction, and its interpretation have expanded to include the interaction between the formerly separated elements—texts, authors, readers, and the cultures that produce them.

It is not surprising, then, that more recently we have become interested in asking why readers resist texts that are culturally unfamiliar to them. This is not to say that readers have always embraced all texts written within their own cultures. Indeed, students' resistance to literary texts is legendary among English teachers. However, resistance as an area of inquiry did not receive attention from either literary theorists or educators until relatively recently. That it is now receiving that attention is largely due to its greater visibility as teachers of literature have expanded the literary canon. As students resist literature that represents diverse ethnic and global cultures, teachers have become concerned for two reasons: (1) Teachers themselves feel they know too little about those cultures and, therefore, do not know what to do about the vocalization of students' resistance; (2) the fact that students voice their resistance to the literature of traditionally underrepresented groups (Beach, 1997) in particular has made teachers aware that their classrooms are not the homogeneous communities they rightly or wrongly believed they were. As Rogers (1997) found in her study of an interpretive community in an urban high school, they are just as likely to be "sites of struggle" as "sites of consensus" (p. 97). When we explore the meaning of *culture* in actual classroom settings, we find, more often than not, that it cannot be conceived of as a monolithic term (Trimmer & Warnock, 1992), whether in reference to our own culture or to other cultures. Trimmer and Warnock (1992) suggest that instead we adopt a view of culture as having "multiple meanings"; in doing so, we are able to speculate about how "words and worlds interact" and "how this interaction create[s] cultural contexts" (p. vii). Thus, our inquiry broadens to include questions that invite readers to consider how they perceive texts to be representative of cultures and the "roles that our own ethnicities, gender, race and class play in that representation" (Trimmer & Warnock, 1992, p. vii).

There is no blueprint for the kinds of investigations suggested by these issues. A rhetorical approach might be utilized to explore narrative strategies in texts across cultures. We might draw upon experiential theories of reader response (Beach, 1991) to help students understand their possible resistance to literature drawn from their own as well as other cultures. We might examine the role of other texts in the creation and structure of the literary text under scrutiny (e.g., the use of culture-specific mythologies). We might also deconstruct our own readings of texts representative of other cultures. And, in this brief catalogue of possibilities, we could also consider locating *significance* through the lens of the functions writers perceive themselves to have in cultures producing the texts we are reading.

On Resistance and Culturally Situated Response

As all of us who teach know, student resistance to literary texts cuts across cultural boundaries. As stated earlier in this chapter, many young adults, initiates as they are in the literary community, resist literary texts more often than not. However, being aware of our reading habits as *predispositions* that determine how we interpret what we read and how they influence our abilities to respond enables us to enter the reading of literature of other cultures alert to the possibility that we may not be able to read as we customarily do when reading texts representative of our own cultural frames of reference.

Resistance may arise in response to *content* and, thus, to attitudes and values embedded in the content (Soter, 1997). With respect to content, unfamiliar attitudes and values embodied in characters or narrators may challenge readers to explore what they perceive as inviolate and cherished, including beliefs that "we're all the same" (Beach, 1997, p. 78). Readers may also react negatively to characters who challenge stereotypical views (e.g., "I thought Chinese women were always demure").

Resistance may also arise in response to form (Rogers & Soter, 1997; Soter, 1997). With respect to form, resistance may occur when narrative patterns do not conform to those we are familiar with (whether written by writers of other cultures or not). Readers may also respond resistantly to texts that challenge their assumptions as to what constitutes "fiction" and what does not. For example, some of my adult students find it difficult to enter Avi's novel, *Nothing but the Truth* (1991), written as it is in the form of a dramatic script. Their perceptions of what constitutes a "novel" were violated, and yet they could not read the text as a "play."

I do not hold the view that resistance (aesthetic or otherwise) is unnatural. Rather, I see it as a natural manifestation of what occurs in the face of the unfamiliar in *any* context of human behavior. The issue is not whether it should not manifest itself; rather, it *will* manifest, and the task of the teacher is to understand its source and then help readers to work their way through it. Dasenbrook's (1992) use of Davidson's concept of "interpretive charity" is useful here. Instead of assuming "difference," Davidson suggests we assume "similitude" (quoted in Dasenbrook, 1992, p. 40)—and if this does not work, to develop a "passing theory" (quoted in Dasenbrook, 1992, p. 40) that will enable us to work toward an acceptance and "understanding of difference" (quoted in Dasenbrook, 1992, p. 40). If we can accomplish this phase, communication across the area of *difference* is possible. As Dasenbrook (1992) argues, it is not so much a case of sharing a set of beliefs, practices, and values as a matter of understanding what others mean, even if we do not know what those beliefs, practices, and values are. The strength of this argument lies in its potential for enabling us to "change . . . adapt, learn in the encounter with the anomalous" (p. 40), which, in turn, "causes changes in the interpretive system of the interpreter" (Dasenbrook, 1992, p. 41). Thus, reading becomes a "model of learning" rather than a "scene of possession, of the demonstration of knowledge already in place" (Dasenbrook, 1992, p. 39).

In this chapter I will address what we take into account when we read outside our own cultures and how an understanding of reading as an activity that involves cultural practices, attitudes, and values may help us understand why our students respond as they do to these and other texts. I have selected two young adult novels for this discussion: Walter Dean Myers's *Somewhere in the Darkness* (1992) (African American) and Shizuko Go's *Requiem* (1985) (Japanese). A brief synopsis of each novel is provided prior to its discussion from an outsider's and, in the case of *Requiem*, an insider's perspective. Myers's novel was selected because it is situated in the United States but yet represents issues that readers remain hesitant to claim familiarity with. On the other hand, Go's novel was selected because it represents a way of life and attitudes that many in the West are not familiar with. A brief synopsis of both novels follows.

WALTER DEAN MYERS'S *SOMEWHERE IN THE DARKNESS*: A SYNOPSIS

After his mother's death and, later, his father's imprisonment for theft and murder, Jimmy Little, almost 15, lives in New York with Mama Jean, his aunt and unofficial foster parent. When we first meet him, he appears to be drifting, often missing school, watching TV and hanging out with two other truant friends. He loves and respects Mama Jean and does not wish to deceive her about going to school, but although he is regarded as a bright student and has done well with his studies, he seems to have lost his desire to continue to do so. This is the scenario when Cephus Little (Jimmy's father)—or Crab, as he prefers to be known—escapes from prison and appears at Mama Jean's apartment to claim Jimmy. Crab does not admit that he is on the run. He claims that he wants time with his family (Jimmy) and has plans for a job in Chicago. Jimmy does not want to go with him—as far as he knows, his father murdered some people in an armed robbery. Although he accepts Crab's assertion of innocence, he does not believe it. Nevertheless, he must go with his father, a man he neither likes nor respects. The rest of the novel traces their journey from New York to Chicago and then to Memphis. By the time the authorities finally catch up with Crab in Memphis, Jimmy has come to terms with his father as someone who has made some bad decisions in his life but who is, essentially, not a bad person. He can accept that, in his own way, Crab is trying to make up for all his failures with his son and society in general. When Crab is caught, Jimmy also learns why his father needed to make amends with him—Crab has advanced TB and, therefore, will not heal from a gunshot wound and loss of blood incurred during his capture. The novel ends with Jimmy's return to New York and the suggestion of renewed purpose in his life.

Resistance from Within: A Discussion

Perhaps strangely, a greater challenge in honoring plurality and accepting the unfamiliar may come from reading literature that represents other cultural groups *within* the United States rather than cultures separated from us by oceans. This is the case despite considerable knowledge about cultural groups within the United States and despite constant interaction with individuals who represent them.

On the other hand, we can often respond more spontaneously to what we did not formerly know precisely because it is unfamiliar and because our prior experiences do not alert us to a potential challenge to our biases. Dasenbrook (1992) expands on this paradox when he recalls his 4-year-old son's "rapt attention of someone utterly engrossed in his first opera," suggesting that "the unknown can be powerful *precisely* because it is unknown" (pp. 39–40). He argues that we

> must remember that knowledge does not come first; the *experience of the work comes first* and leads the experiencer to the knowledge . . . therefore, it is *not* the expert reader who counts but the reader *willing* to become an expert. (p. 40; emphases added)

Beach (1997) proposes that rather than focus on the use of multicultural literature as a means of changing attitudes, we should concentrate on what beliefs and attitudes students bring to class with them as a way of beginning connections with the literature itself. That is, we should assume biases and resistance and, in doing so, begin with discussions about these rather than assuming that simply reading literature of other cultures will somehow make students osmotically receptive to those cultures and their values. Hines's research (1997) also suggests that allowing for "multiplicities in response" (p. 124) may not only help reduce resistance but bring about an understanding of its nature and origin.

If we come to reading as Jauss (quoted in Godzich, 1994) argues—"carrying with us a whole world of familiar beliefs and expectations" (p. 41)—then *Somewhere in the Darkness* can, at one level, be read as a stereotypical novel about the relationship of a young, urban African American and his seemingly deadbeat dad, whom he finally meets after his father's escape from prison:

> They lived on the fourth floor of a seven-storied building. The elevator didn't work, and the owner had boarded up the stairs at the top of the fifth floor. Sometimes he could hear people going past the fifth floor. Once a month the superintendent would get the cops to go up and chase away the junkies, but they would always come back. (p. 7)

That Jimmy has been living with Mama Jean since his mother's death and his father's apparent abandonment of his family suggests a recognizable, stereotypical pattern. Similarly stereotypical is the following: He is bright but failing school; he feels alienated from most of his friends because he no longer dreams of doing well in school in order to escape ghetto life; he often pretends to go to school but spends most of the day at the movies. When the school psychologist interviews him, he asks:

> "What we're wondering . . . is why someone of your intelligence is doing so badly in school?" (p. 5)

To this, he merely shrugs; and in response to questions about his father, he creates a fiction of a man who works in a bus garage checking buses and with whom he "gets on alright" (p. 6). However, before we are too long into the novel, Myers takes us *inside* his character, and the stereotypical exterior begins to blur. We see a young man struggling to understand why he lacks energy to do anything:

> Jimmy hadn't been sick so much as he had been tired. . . . It seemed to come from *inside*. It was almost as if something tired was growing in him. In the

mornings he would just get up and not feel like doing anything. He didn't know why. (p. 17; emphasis added)

Had Jimmy gone to a psychiatrist, he would most probably have been diagnosed as being seriously depressed. His aimless drifting, his indifference to what others think (even the grandmother he loves), and his inertia convey a sense of hopelessness that brings him much closer to us. Is it the author who leads us out of what could be read as a stereotypical story, to a reading that, instead, challenges us to see the story as a "scene of learning" (Dasenbrook, 1992, p. 39)? If so, we assume that the author has used some strategey that overcomes our possible resistance to go against the grain. Some of my students were able to move from resistance to an acceptance that this story was more than just a typical story of the struggles and hardships faced by an urban African American boy and his family. It seems that Myers's shift from the *exterior to the interior* altered their views of the novel in a way that upset their preconceived beliefs that it would simply confirm urban stereotypes. By moving the reader into Jimmy's interior world, Myers effects a narrative turn that is essential for our empathetic involvement throughout the rest of the novel. Myers cannot afford to have us be distanced from Jimmy if we are to retain our connection with him for the duration of the fictional journey. When we first meet Crab, we see him as Jimmy sees him and feel the same anger, sense of betrayal, and shame that he feels. As the novel progresses and Jimmy leaves with Crab to drive to Chicago and later, to Marion, West Memphis (Crab's home town), we find ourselves empathizing with Crab and able to see him as someone who has lost his way, because Jimmy has begun his own journey to compassion:

"It don't make a difference if you didn't kill nobody. . . . Not if you're going to steal some money or credit cards or something. That's wrong too. It don't make you good just because you didn't kill nobody!" (p. 155)

Jimmy also struggles to *hear* Crab *despite* the judgment:

Jimmy searching his face for meaning beyond what he would say, knowing that he might not trust anything that was just words. (p. 155)

This is followed by his final outburst in response to Crab's reasoning as to why Jimmy *should* listen to him ("Can't I just be your father. . . . I am your father"), which brings to the surface the "naked truth that Crab did not indeed know how to be a father" (p. 156) and acts cathartically—for how can we blame someone who does not know? Yet in that moment of recognition also lies the knowledge of what could have been, and this brings forgiveness, enabling Jimmy to know that when Crab must run one final time, he, Jimmy, can release him with forgiveness. With that comes recognition and an acceptance of the nature of their relationship despite all the surface appearances to the contrary and despite Jimmy's earlier assertion that Crab "don't know enough to be a father"; he acknowledges Crab *is* his father, and as Crab lies, shot, trying to apologize, Jimmy is finally able to say, "I know, Daddy. . . . I know" (p. 161).

One of Myers's strengths in what Sims Bishop (1991) terms his "urban reality novels" is his "ability to create believable, sympathetic characters" (p. 65). The narrative craft that accomplishes this rendering in *Somewhere in the Darkness* is a consequence of choosing Jimmy as the vehicle for bringing about understanding and sympathy toward Crab in the reader. We are with Jimmy from the first encounter with Crab—judging him, seeing him as a con artist, as a liar, as a man prepared to duck responsibility at every level and as a man who cannot face himself as he is. Yet (and because) as Jimmy learns more about him and, finally, comes to forgive him and accept him as he is, so do we. The effect is *not* a sentimental, fairy-tale ending, because we have been part of the struggle. Given "interpretive charity" (Dasenbrook, 1992, p. 39), we find that these are not just issues faced by urban African Americans but issues we all have to face in one way or other: Who am I in relation to who my father or mother is? What is our relation to each other? And the most difficult question (because answers are always so elusive): What is most important in my life? Jimmy answers that question by asking himself what he would want for his own child, especially if that child were a boy. His answer is one we can all connect with:

> He would tell him all the secrets he knew, looking right into his eyes and telling him nothing but the truth so that every time they were together they would know things about each other. That way there would be a connection. . . . He knew that if he ever had a son he would have to do it right away, and all the time, because sooner or later there wouldn't be enough days left to fit the meaning in. (p. 167)

However, because it is also a novel written by an African American author, it presents us with the challenge of facing our view of the urban African American ghetto stereotype. I have found students strongly resistant to acknowledging its "African Americanness." They will not write about this and will not discuss this aspect of the novel and tend to "avoid thoughtful discussion of issues of race and class" (Beach, 1997, p. 69). In contrast, they are much more accepting of features they identify as "Japanese" in Go's novel, perhaps suggestive of Beach's (1997) argument that some students "respond to portrayals of racial difference with a voyeuristic fascination . . . a contrast to their own middle-class suburban worlds

. . . which often leads to a false substitute for grappling with authentic portrayals of racial difference" (p. 79).

Even this powerfully evocative and well-crafted novel, however, does not overcome all resistance when that resistance is grounded in cultural stereotypes. Some students, understandably, were not able to assume that they would learn something from their encounter with this novel and its characters. Because the initial assumption was one of negative difference, they were unable to go through the process that Dasenbrook (1992) suggests we need to encourage students to go through if they are to accept difference as a positive phenomenon. That is, the process described earlier, whereby we initially assume similarity as our first "theory" (p. 40). Such an assumption suggests receptivity to what we might not know (difference). That, in turn, would enable us to incorporate what we perceive as "anomalous information" into our understanding about poor African American urban youth—information, that is, which we would otherwise reject if we did not begin with what Dasenbrook (1992) describes as "interpretive charity" (p. 39).

SHIZUKO GO'S *REQUIEM*

Synopsis

Shizuko Go's *Requiem* (1985) begins in an air-raid shelter in Yokohama as Setsuko, the protagonist, awakens on yet another night, alone and seriously ill. Her family and friends have all died in the incendiary raids on the city during the latter stages of World War II. The novel consists of a series of recollections through remembered letters, journal entries, and conversations as Setsuko fades in and out of consciousness. We do not have a typical plot sequence, for the heroine can no longer act. Throughout the entire novel, she is, in fact, lying in the otherwise abandoned air-raid shelter near her former home. She is too weak to move, can barely see, and is often delirious. She can only reconstruct the past in fragments.

It is a powerfully moving story told through the eyes of a sympathetic but absent narrator. Through Setsuko's recollections, we hear about the division in Japan among those who supported the imperial war effort and those who did not. As Setsuko struggles to make sense of the disaster around her, the loss of her family, and, as far as she knows, all her friends, she also struggles with her own feelings of patriotism, questioning their validity in the face of total destruction. We join her as she recalls conversations with her friend, Wakui, who argued that the war would end and that to continue to sacrifice their lives for their country and emperor would be meaningless. Hajime, her brother, made the sacrifice, Setsuko recalls. The most difficult memories are related to her school friend, Naomi. Despite their separation as the war continued (Japanese schoolgirls were withdrawn from school and sent to work in factories and farms to support the war effort), they remained in touch. Although strained, their friendship also survived Setsuko's patriotic support for the war effort, while Naomi's father was imprisoned for his criticism of it. It was not until Setsuko had decided to visit Naomi and found the latter's house burned to ashes from an incendiary raid that she had admitted the cause of the rift in their friendship: Setsuko knew that she had never fully accepted Naomi's stance on the war and, more important, that Naomi knew this and yet loved her despite it. But Setsuko can never ask forgiveness now. As the war nears its end, so does Setsuko's life. The thread of memories is maintained down to the last moment as Setsuko takes her final breath. Peering out of the shelter, barely able to see, she perceives against the skyline a figure she deliriously takes for her brother, Hajime. As she slips into her "deepest sleep," the reader knows that it is not Hajime but "an American soldier—one of the very first to land in Japan"; but Setsuko has already "slid down the shelter floor. She would never move again" (p. 122).

Resistance from Without: A Discussion

My discussion of this novel centers around the responses students have had to it and provides another example of how what a teacher might perceive to be a very powerful, moving literary experience could be strongly resisted by students because it upsets some very cherished convictions, even among those considered "insiders" of the culture. For example, patriotism is something that we accord to ourselves, not to the enemy. It is something only the "good guys" feel when called upon to support and defend their country. As one student wrote:

> It was quite shocking for me to read about Setsuko's seemingly unquestioned patriotism and devotion to her country. . . . I believe this is also a strong defense mechanism that enables one to better live with the knowledge of that past without still suffering a great deal from it

Later, in her paper, this student revealed the reason for her difficulty in dealing with her struggle to view Setsuko's patriotism:

> I must relate a rather painful piece from my personal history. My father-in-law served in the United States Navy during the Second

World War, stationed on a ship in the South Pacific. . . . As my husband tells me, he and his fellow soldiers naturally viewed the Japanese as the enemy, a belief which . . . he could not overcome throughout the remainder of his life.

She went on to say:

Thus I approached *Requiem* with a very odd mixture of emotional and intellectual baggage. At the outset of the novel, I feared that the story would focus on the victims of the atomic bombs dropped on Hiroshima or Nagasaki, another controversial topic among us Americans. . . . However, I was previously unknowledgeable about the extent to which the rest of Japan was bombed using conventional warfare, and was disturbed to learn about the bombing of the civilian population as related in the book.

This initial resistance and careful reconnoitering around a sensitive topic gave way to an appreciation for what this student had not known before: (1) the extensive bombing of civilians and (2) the revelation that Japanese civilians were also in conflict about the war, some imprisoned and alienated because of their objections to it.

Other aspects of the novel that students had greater difficulty connecting with included Setsuko's strong wish for a quick death. Students searched the novel for evidence that there were good reasons why she might want to die. As one student wrote:

Her emotional anguish at losing her father and living with an alcoholic, mentally ill mother for whom she had to act as a parent might explain her wish to die.

Others felt that Setsuko's inability "to see the larger picture" caused her to lose hope. Still others commented that from the very beginning of the novel, "resistance might be expected" because,

the protagonist is so unlike the readers, the book starts on a somber note and goes down from there, and the theme is not something readers particularly want to deal with. . . . When we do address the less than uplifting stories, we at least have a strong moral message to hold onto at the end and an identifiable bad guy to hate. . . . Go denies us this.

One "insider," a young Japanese woman taking the course, had quite a different view of the novel. According to Junko,

In Japanese society, harmony is esteemed in many respects. During the war especially, it was a great principle for all people to fight for their nation. In such circumstances, it was very noteworthy [of Setsuko] to support the girl [Naomi] marked as the daughter of an unpatriotic person.

Junko argued that this is *not*

simply an anti-war novel for, if the author had aimed to draw this novel to describe the horrors of war, the novel's *protagonist* should have been *Naomi* [not Setsuko], whose father was imprisoned for a crime of thought. And Naomi herself appealed to Setsuko about the horrible war by writing things like "I wish with all my heart I'd been born in an age without war. Why do people go to war when we're all the same human beings?" (p. 121)

Another Japanese student, Aki, disagreed with Junko's assertion that Naomi should have been the protagonist. According to Aki, Setsuko's role as protagonist is what makes this a powerful anti-war novel. Her struggle with the concept of "unquestioned patriotism" is the heart of the novel. Aki also suggested that "the sense of loss . . . the emptiness, which most Japanese people felt when they knew they could not trust what they had believed in their whole life . . . disoriented them." She also believes that this "disorientedness" is still prevalent in Japan today and prompted Go to write the novel because:

Japanese leaders may consider World War II a great fault in Japanese history, but I believe they think that the last war was a fault because we lost, not because of the nature of war itself. Of course, most Japanese people do not share this idea, but leaders could not change this point of view, for if they did, they wouldn't have anything to hold onto, a strength to revive this country.

Aki believes that Japanese people today have still not resolved their stance toward World War II and that the unresolved ending of the novel reflects Go's desire to foreground this:

I think Go did not write about what happens after Setsuko died, because the questions many Japanese still have in mind haven't been solved yet—the questions about what we can trust and what we can make of the last war. In this sense, World War II hasn't ended in many people's minds. . . . To me, *Requiem* was powerful because it made me realize that we still have unfinished business and it gave us a question to think about: What should we do now?

Aki further stated that "it is typical Japanese style to not have a clear ending to a novel" because "the sense of incompleteness makes readers think about the issues in the novel. Japanese readers," said Aki, "traditionally appreciate the echoes or the lingering tones which they can feel after the reading."

Junko further revealed that "Japanese students today are ignorant of the war and not taught the war history in high school because Japanese leaders consider World War II as a great fault in Japanese history because they don't want to pay indemnities to former Japanese colonies." She further pointed out that during the year in which *Requiem* was published, Okinawa was returned to Japan by the United States and the resulting problems in handling defense were being discussed at the time of publication.

Some of my non-Japanese students had commented that they were troubled with the death of not only Setsuko but of every major character she had introduced to us. Junko noted that although she felt sad after reading the novel, and that this response might well have been induced by the "predominance of death" in the novel, readers should "*not* feel a sense of dread." "If anything," she says, "death is considered as a beautiful figure in this novel." Aki concurred, adding that:

> It is not that the Japanese choose to die easily. Because they know that life is precious, it is considered to be the best way of showing their loyalty by committing suicide. . . . Setsuko did not commit suicide but adhered to the Japanese notion to fight to the last as a Japanese . . . and thus, readers are left with ambiguity, which signifies the current state of Japan.

According to Junko, literary critics in Japan were not kind to the author when the novel was first published (1972) in Japanese. They saw it as labored, long, and amateurish, and, according to Junko, they felt "betrayed when Setsuko dies," describing it as a "cheap trick to make the story a tragedy." She further disclosed that even the harshest critics of the novel recognized that it might have been written as a response to the "recent militaristic movement in Japan, which alarmed the author"—who may therefore have felt moved to "reflect on her own experience during the war."

Despite their resistance to the novel in the ways described, my students responded empathetically to Setsuko's fiercely honest struggle and appreciated that the author did not evade truths, unpleasant though they might be. It is left to one of the minor characters, recalled by Setsuko when close to her end, to express a hope that many of my students found matched their own:

> "I've been thinking lately that to the people, individually, war is like a storm. It arrives unwanted, smashes into their lives, and then suddenly blows over. We, the people, are the ones who sustain and carry on the war, but we're not the ones who begin it or end it." (pp. 114–115)

In drawing OUT responses to *Somewhere in the Darkness* and *Requiem* together, a striking difference emerged in the patterns of resistance to them; that is, the resistances to the Japanese text were explicitly stated and those to the African American text were not. As noted earlier, many students were reluctant to even discuss *Somewhere in the Darkness*. Perhaps we are, after all, more willing to suspend our disbelief in the face of the exotic rather than the familiar, as Beach (1997) has suggested. However, choosing to exclude those texts that will be met with silence will not help students move beyond stereotypes or develop an understanding of how those stereotypes are constructed.

APPLICATIONS OF CULTURALLY SITUATED RESPONSES TO OTHER YOUNG ADULT NOVELS

In discussing a novel written by a writer from outside the United States and another by a writer who is very much a part of the fabric of life within the United States and yet still regarded by many as representative of another distinct culture within the country, I intended to illustrate some of the challenges we will encounter in the classroom as we attempt to generate a dialogue between students and literary readings representative of other cultures. The *insider/outsider* perspective makes explicit the relationships we have with the cultures represented in these texts but *does not overcome* potential obstacles to engagement. As many scholars and researchers in the field of literacy argue, extensive exposure to literature that is representative of a diversity of cultures both within and outside the United States is critical if we are to help students adjust their "horizons of expectations" (Jauss, 1982, p. 24). However, exposure alone is not a sufficient condition for engagement.

Greater familiarity with diversity in literature, as in life, may, however, eventually create greater tolerance for the strange or the unfamiliar. Some excellent anthologies of short fiction as well as novels are now available in the field of young adult literature. Among these are collections of Hispanic American, African American, Asian American, and Native American short stories, notably Joyce Carol Thomas's anthology, *A Gathering of Flowers* (1990), and Anne Mazer's *America Street: A Multicultural Anthology of Stories* (1993). Hazel Rochman's edited collection, *Somehow Tenderness Survives* (1988), contains a variety of African writers of various nationalities, among them Mark Mathabene, Doris Lessing, Nadine Gordimer, Gcina Mhlope, and Ernst Havemann. Linda Crew and Lawrence Yep's fiction focuses on how Cambodian and Chinese young adults adjust to life in the United States while maintaining ties with their parents' home cultures. Walter Dean Myers's *Fallen Angels* (1988) presents older students with challenging questions of loyalty and patriotism among young African American soldiers who fought in Vietnam before they were old enough to vote.

The voices of "the other" have begun to proliferate in the field of young adult literature. The challenging of long-held assumptions about what constitutes "a good story" has likewise begun among readers who cannot call upon their customary reading preferences to determine what these other voices mean. Nor can we, teachers, necessarily rely on our own reading and life experiences to make sense of literature that for many of us also represents "uncharted (if exciting) trails" (Soter, 1997, p. 227).

We are back, then, to a view of the literary experience as a "scene of learning" (Dasenbrook, 1992, p. 42), a view that surely applies to the reading of any literature but that is particularly applicable to the reading of the literature of other cultures. The following questions and suggested activities are grounded in that view. Readers will also recognize their links to cultural criticism and reader response theories.

QUESTIONS AND ACTIVITIES FOR FURTHER EXPLORATION

Questions

Questions we might ask concerning how we should read texts representative of other cultures, whether within or outside the United States, include the following:

1. Are the critical lenses we are used to wearing appropriate and even useful when reading texts written by Native American, African, Hispanic, and African American writers? Can our traditional understanding of what constitutes "narrative" help us understand the rhetorical effects of literature of other cultures?

2. What is the nature of our resistance, and what in the text triggers it?
3. In what ways are readers naive when journeying through these texts? What kinds of boundaries (e.g., favored beliefs and attitudes) are being challenged by reading these texts?
4. How is our resistance to these texts the same as or different from the re-sistance we might have to literature from our own tradition?
5. What do we find we share in common with the characters and their situ-ations in texts written by writers of other cultures?
6. What do we find, in terms of our reading habits and preferences, that we cannot rely on as we navigate these texts?
7. What alternative aesthetic models, if any, seem to be functioning in these texts?

Activities

The insider/outsider perspective is especially suited to the study of literature as a field of inquiry. The following are some suggestions for application:

1. Students could take the role of anthropologists with one or more texts, shifting the focus from their own response to an inquiry that begins with the assumption that the "community" to be studied is relatively unknown, although of interest. Involved in such a study would be the use of cul-tural informants who would confirm or disconfirm the student anthro-pologists' assumptions and interpretations. The result of such a project could be a "thrice-told tale" (Wolf, 1992) consisting of three parts: (1) Students could write field notes as they record their initial observations in their early encounters with the text, which are then responded to by selected cultural informants who might even be class members; (2) they could construct an account of the text as a biography; (3) they would then write a formal report written with the whole class as the intended audi-ence and present it as an exhibition piece.
2. Students could be asked to record in two columns (one labeled "insider perspective" and the other "outsider perspective") elements of a text that they regard as ones that require insider knowledge versus elements that they believe any reader (i.e., including outsiders) could identify. In dis-cussion, their choices could be explained in terms of how students see themselves placed in relation to the culture represented in the novel.
3. Teachers might follow up the previous activity by asking students to con-sider which question they would ask the author of the text, which, in turn, would enable them to better understand the cultural group de-picted in the novel and clarify any ambiguity or uncertainty they had experienced in reading the text that could be attributed to lacking insider knowledge.

When using novels written by writers of other cultures (within and outside the United States) I have found that adopting the insider/outsider frame has enabled students to overcome some of their resistance related to guilt or to a fear of social repercussions when expressing views they believe are not perceived as politically correct. However, a lifetime of habitual thinking and values cannot be eradicated with the experience of one or two novels that challenge the preconceptions of the reader. We serve our students' interests better if we *bring resistance into our classroom discussions as integrally related to the interpretive experience.* In itself, resistance is not the interesting issue; rather, what is of interest is how we use it.

Why resistance?
Do authors expect this?
What can we do with it?

CHAPTER 8

Putting It All Together: From Reader to Text to Reader

The distance between personal response and critical analysis is not as wide as has often been thought. In the preceding chapters, my discussions of novels from one critical perspective or other proceeded in each case from a *personal* connection with them. Each text appeared to invite analysis from the critical perspective chosen; however, *another reader* may have received an alternative invitation. Granted, a novice literary reader may perceive fewer interpretive options than an experienced one, and in the case of the seasoned literary reader, response and analysis may even have merged so that one appears indistinguishable from the other. However,

> what each reader makes of the text, is indeed for *him*, the poem, in the sense that this is his only direct interpretation of it. No one else can read it for him. He may learn indirectly about others' experiences with the text; he may come to see that his own was confused or impoverished, and he may then be stimulated to attempt to call forth from the text a better poem. But this he must do himself, and only what he himself experiences in relation to the text is—again let us underline—*for him*, the work. (Rosenblatt, 1978, p. 105; emphasis in original)

In honoring response, Rosenblatt (1978) claims that we acknowledge as valid the "uniquely personal character of literary experience" and discover "how in *this situation* critical discrimination and sound criteria of interpretation can be achieved" (Rosenblatt, 1978, p. 105; emphasis added). That is, we see response and criticism as embedded in one another rather than as the separate phenomena we traditionally maintained they are.

Rosenblatt (1978) did not perceive reader response theory as a "soft option" or an avoidance of the kind of hard thinking we have come to associate with literary criticism. Rather, she sees readers as capable of reflection and possessing a degree of objectivity that enables them to understand the relationships that inevitably occur among themselves, the literary texts they read, and the authors who created them. Her view of readers responding to texts is a transactional one that respects the role of each in the interpretive process.

However, some scholars (e.g., Miller, 1986) have distinguished reading (and the subjective response to it) as private and criticism as public activities. According to Leitch (1992), by designating reading as private, we implicitly suggest that it *precedes* the public act of criticism and, in doing so, elevate criticism to a place where it is presumed to be "uncontaminated by personal interests, prejudices, values or blind spots" (p. 110). What this view avoids is the admission that although *personal* interests, prejudices, and values may be suppressed in the practice of criticism, *group* interests, prejudices, and values are *not*. As Leitch (1992) observes, "It is a well-attested cliche that the functioning of social groups is invariably shaped by values, which means that certain operative and guiding needs, beliefs, interests, and practices more or less permeate and propel social activities, choices, plans, ideas, customs, and institutions" (p. 1). Criticism, then, is about discussing literary texts in preferred ways that demonstrate mastery over preferred "linguistic, cultural and literary conventions and practices" (Leitch, 1992, p. 110).

The primary distinctions between response and criticism have depended on the extent to which the interpretations of naive readers have been compared to the more elaborate and technically sophisticated ones made by more mature readers. However, if we acknowledge that readers have an integral role to play in the interpretive process, we cannot ignore *who* those readers are and, in doing that, cannot argue that one kind of reader is better than another. Readers are who they are, situated in their own histories, personalities, and proclivities. To assert that it is better to be sophisticated readers denies, for example, the age and experience of all possible readers. More significantly, unless they fit a particular model of an ideal reader, they will always be perceived as imperfect readers. They will "misread" (Richards, 1929, p. 237) the text.

An alternative approach is to focus, instead, on what our students' responses *tell* us rather than on what they *do not tell* us. This approach is reflected in the response studies of Rogers (1997), Fairbanks (1995), Hynds (1990), and Gibson (1990) in classrooms from kindergarten through college. In pursuing this path in my own classrooms, I have found that students *can* recognize differences between an uninformed, unquestioned response and a considered, informed critical response. I have also found that students are capable of "multiplicities of response" (Hines, 1997). That is, literary works are responded to in multiple ways depending on the texts, where the same student is in relation to the texts, and how the text itself invites the student to engage with it. Sometimes, too, students are not ready to "explicate." When the initial response is particularly powerful, they often find it difficult to articulate that response in an immediate way. This should not be surprising if we examine our own responses to books we approach as readers rather than as teachers. As Dorin Schumacher (1989) states, "Literary critics, unless they are advocates of a special school of criticism, are not accustomed to examining and revealing their assumptions and methods but tend simply to present the *results* of their criticism" (p. 36; emphasis added).

If this book were not concerned with how we can help young readers make sense of their own connections with the literature they read, my concern with distinctions between response and criticism might seem superfluous. After all, I have dedicated much of this book to various forms of critical explication. However, woven throughout those explications is always my subjective position, my private connection to the texts. Where does pure response end and pure criticism begin? Could it not be the case that neither is *pure* but, rather, is simply a different expression of the same basic phenomenon—that is, *a reading?*

As my discussion in the next section will show, I initially made an arbitrary distinction between response and criticism in my analysis of some student responses. Underlying this interest was my view that there seemed to be a continuum of response to criticism in their work as well as a blending of both practices. However, after these categories were applied, I found, as Bogdan (1992) did, that the distinctions between categories were arbitrary and limiting. Furthermore, defining what constitutes "response" and "criticism" is troubling, in effect assuming that my students should have responded in some other, more appropriate way.[1] Therefore, I became more interested in the *intrepretive range* that their comments displayed. As a result, I also began to question my initial view of response and criticism as representing a continuum; rather, I saw what my students wrote as suggestive of an *interplay* between response and criticism. I concluded, as Bogdan (1992) did, that response might be viewed as another way of knowing the literary text, in her words, "an alternative perspective which involves a different set of values and a different system of noticings and unnoticings, transferring imaginative energy from life to literature rather than the other way round" (p. 264). In more recent work, Bogdan, Dark, and Robertson (1997) suggest that we enrich classroom experiences with literature when we banish our distinctions, for example, between naive and sophisticated readers, between response and criticism, and between "high" and "low" literature (p. 82). It is with Rosenblatt (1978) and both Bogdan (1992) and Bogdan and colleagues (1997) in mind that I want now to turn attention to how we might view reader response as *more* than just a starting point for helping students become the sophisticated, knowing, learned readers of literary text we typically hope they will become. I want to argue

---

1. For this insight I am indebted to Deane Bogdan (private conversation, August, 1998).

that criticism as we have known and practiced it is, in essence, a *formalization of particular kinds of response* that reflect *preferred* ways of knowing and sharing information about literary texts.

=cont, not a response

THE ARTIFICIAL CONSTRUCT: RESPONSE TYPES ON A CONTINUUM

In the process of teaching courses in young adult literature, I developed a series of assignments that culminated in a final paper in which students wrote a response essay on a selected novel followed by a critical analysis of the same novel and a concluding section in which they discussed the comparative strengths and limitations of each approach. Prior to this final assignment, students had also completed other response-based writing as well as read and discussed the novels from a variety of critical perspectives as a way of preparing for the final paper. A secondary purpose in developing this assignment was to provide students with an experience in which they would become aware of the relationships between response and criticism so that they would subsequently know how to interpret the characterstics of their students' responses to literary texts as well as view them as evidence of student *learning,* not just student-friendly activities.

Representative comments from the students indicate that they came to see a closer relationship between personal response and critical analysis as a result of the final assignment:

> In responding personally, I found that I was actually fleshing out many of the critical aspects of the novel without being "critical." I did not analyze the story, but I took time to realize what struck a chord in me. . . . It seemed as though one type of analysis (analyzing my responses) can feed the other (analyzing the text).

Another student observed:

> These two seemingly different perspectives on literature might only represent the extreme ends of a continuum along which different amounts of personal involvement in the poem exist. This suggests that one approach does not exclude the other. . . . I do not think that we are so much trying to create a valid or correct interpretation of the work as we are struggling to create a valid and useful experience out of that complex process known as reading. . . . Perhaps only by contrasting the supposedly objective with the so-called personal can we have the richest [reading] experience.

These comments are typical of those made by the students and resulted in my conducting a more intensive analysis of shifts from response to analysis and a better understanding of relationships between the two that I observed in their work over the period of the course. In the following discussion I briefly describe Bogdan's (1992) categories, using examples drawn from several written responses of several students applying Bogdan's (1992) categories from what seem to be the most subjective responses to those that appear most critical. In doing so, I am establishing the case for viewing response and criticism as a cyclical phenomenon, often inseparable, always reflective of how readers cross the artificial boundaries we attempt to impose. This is followed by a comparison of a novice/expert critique and a brief discussion of how even one student's written response to a text can display the full range of responses (stasis, partial responses, and critical response) that have been discussed.

In my analyses I focused on categorizing students' responses according to whether they suggested *stasis* (Bogdan's [1992] precritical response), *stock and kinetic responses* (partial responses), or *critical responses*. These are now briefly described and illustrated with samples from my students' work.

Stasis

Stasis, says Bogdan (1992), is "the simultaneous perception and experience of the *total form* of the literary work however fleeting that glimpse might be." According to Bogdan, stasis can be thought of as "the apotheosis of *engagement* with the text, its most prominent characteristic being the virtual disappearance of the self-conscious critical faculty." Whatever its cognitive value, stasis "resides in the *instinctual and instantaneous apprehension of and union with* the art object in terms of its imaginative and emotional impact" (p. 113; emphases added). This response sometimes results in silence, an inability or unwillingness to articulate the impact of the work on us. If we are at all conscious of flaws or limitations or disappointments, they do not bother us. In each of the following student examples, we see evidence of the uncritical response that totally embraces the work:

> I loved the book [*Jacob Have I Loved*] and would read it again. Why I loved it is a difficult question to answer.

> I was so caught up in it [*Jacob Have I Loved*] that I just wanted to continue reading it without interruption. I was so moved by the novel that the images did not leave me quickly, and I was genuinely shocked when others who had read the work thought Louise was a whiner and had neither sympathy or empathy for her.

Lois Lowry's *The Giver* is a truly rare literary find; an entertaining, thought-provoking book that you can't put down and don't want to end.

It was Mary Call who grabbed me by the neck and yanked me into the book [*Where the Lilies Bloom*]. As with most books in its category, the book lived beyond its 210th page.

I was seduced by his [Cormier's *The Bumblebee Flies Anyway*] attention to detail . . . like freshwater fish bated by its captor, I was teased and tantalized, then yanked into the story's element of suspense.

The students have completely entered the worlds of the novels—they are the authors' ideal narrative audiences (Rabinowitz, 1976), they have seen themselves in the shoes of the protagonist, they have crossed over, gone behind Scholes's (1989) "looking glass" (p. 27) and found *themselves* in the text. Their language is frequently expansive:

I loved the book

I was so caught up in it

I was so moved by the novel

a truly rare literature find

a . . . book that you can't put down

like a freshwater fish baited by its captor

These readers *work with* the author to make the text come alive as the following examples indicate:

[handwritten marginal note: is this a problem?]

I was genuinely shocked when others who had read the work thought Louise was a whiner

I realized that Walter Dean Myers really does consider audience when he writes

I was teased and tantalized, then yanked along by the story's element of suspense

Although these responses *appear* to reflect an uncritical acceptance of the novels cited, they are the kinds of responses authors dream of. They are also the kinds of responses we imply we would like to hear from students when we declare that one of our goals as literature teachers is to have our students love literature.

The next two categories are partial responses (Bogdan, 1992), which reveal readers who retain some distance, some sense of self in reserve. They have moved from acceptance to judgment, although the reasons for judgment may be based on limited vision or flawed perceptions of the authors' intentions or limited life/literary experience. They may also reflect strong divergence in tastes. We have a sense of minds rather than emotions generating the responses, whether positively or negatively.

Partial Response

Partial response, is, according to Bogdan (1992), usually attributed to readers who are perceived as lacking expertise at making fine discriminations between literature and life, so that they are likely to experience response as a partial form. The two manifestations of partial response, stock and kinetic responses, "*reinforce* what is already known rather than paving the way for what might be known, stock response with respect to the content of the work and kinetic response with respect to the form of the work" (Bogdan, pp. 115–116; emphasis added).

Either form of partial response might occur when readers confront a text that is grounded in an unfamiliar culture (e.g., see my discussion of Shizuko Go's *Requiem* in Chapter 7) or when, for any variety of reasons, the reader's "horizon of expectations" (Jauss, 1982, p. 24) does not prepare him or her for the work in question. That is, partial response may indeed manifest when students encounter the *unfamiliar* in literature, whether in content or form.

Stock Response. Bogdan (1992) defined stock response as one that "comes from the inability or refusal to fuse with the work through a refusal to suspend disbelief, an unwillingness to delay aesthetic gratification that comes only with the expenditure of effort to perceive the total literary form." Some of my English preservice teachers are inclined to react with stock responses to many young adult novels because of their preconceptions that these novels are simple, have clearly identifiable plots, and have superficial themes.

Stock responses often "relate literature to life in a way that is exclusively in terms of the responders' *current* experiences and values" (Bogdan, 1992, p. 117; emphasis added). School-age children often exhibit this kind of response. Stock responses might be positive or negative. The former frequently reveal readers' identification or ability to relate to a character in their situation. The latter often reveal readers' instant dislike, or a mental block, because they consider the story to be trivial or reprehensible or they have become bored because they perceive the story as outdated:

> By connecting with Phillip and Miss Narwin [in Avi's *Nothing but the Truth*], I found myself making connection after connection with the two main characters of the novel. I [also] instantly bonded with Phillip as I found out he was a track runner. I am a track runner. (*Positive*)

> At the start of my reading of *Jane Eyre*, I judged the book by its length and cover, judging it to be a dry, drawn out story. (*Negative*)

> I was able to relate to Charlotte [in Avi's *The True Confessions of Charlotte Doyle*] from my own childhood experiences. I knew what she was feeling and understood the exhilaration that she must have felt as she scampered across the ropes doing her job. (*Positive*)

> So many parents in today's society back their children and get upset with the school systems before they know both sides of the story. Many of the situations in this book [Avi's *Nothing but the Truth*] could have been eliminated if there would have been some better communication. (*Positive*)

Whether positive or negative, stock responses frequently include phrases such as "I found myself relating to," "I found myself making connections to," or "It reminded me of," as readers make "value judgements about the truth or falsity of literary statements as though they applied to real life or real people" (Bogdan, 1992, p. 116). Patterns in the following examples reveal themselves as connections but also having some distance from the work:

> As the plot developed . . . I found myself eagerly awaiting the next meeting of Jane and Rochester

> The physical island that Wil found and needed, I also found myself relating to strongly

> Charlotte Doyle makes me remember that time when I was a little girl

I instantly [also] bonded with Phillip as I found out he was a track runner. I am a track runner.

We could describe these responses as evidence that these readers have not entered the ideal narrative audience (Rabinowitz, 1976) and in contrast to the stasis-type response, as more restrained in tone. Evaluation is made on the basis of how well the text affirms (or not) the experience of "truth" that is held by the reader. The text is co-constructed according to the extent that its "reality" matches or does not match that of the reader.

Kinetic Response. According to Bogdan (1992), kinetic responses come from "simply wanting literature to 'work' for the reader on a superficial aesthetic level, as entertainment only" (p. 177). These may again be positive and negative, as well as "predictor" and "idealogue" responses (p. 177). The positive kinetic responder views dialogue and characterization as a kind of TV sitcom "imitation of life," deriving pleasure mainly from an uncritical acceptance of what they see and hear (p. 118). Negative kinetic responses are often expressed as complaints about perceived formal deficiencies, such as weak plots, choppiness, superfluousness, and an "unsatisfying ending" (Bogdan, 1992, p. 118).

Predictor kinetic response prevents full engagement with the literary work because these readers are so "self-conscious that [they] jump the gun on the author"; for example, "not another Updike ending" (Bogdan, p. 116). Here literary knowledge is perceived as inhibiting the literary experience through the inhibition of "imaginative engagement" (Bogdan, 1992, p. 116). The idealogue kinetic response inhibits full response because of an entrenched mindset, but here the barrier against the aesthetic mechanism is constructed by "extra-literary knowledge" or belief systems (Bogdan, 1992, p. 119). One might hear, for example, feminist objections to a male character's sexism or male objections to a female character's portrayal. In other words, response is "pushed back a priori" (p. 119). A selection of examples follow:

Avi begins by directly addressing the reader through Charlotte Doyle. Immediately, I knew that this was a narrative account of events that had already transpired and that Charlotte had survived but been somehow changed. (*Positive*)

Two of the three novels seem to have the same style of ending and this is a style I personally enjoy. Both books [Avi's *Nothing but the Truth* and *The True Confessions of Charlotte Doyle*] allow the reader to make predictions, but the final outcome is usually far off the actual prediction. (*Positive*)

I am not sure I liked the ending of the book [Paterson's *Lyddie*]. I really would have liked Lyddie to end up with Luke Stevens so she would have someone there for her. (*Negative*)

First, I do not know of any high school runners [in Avi's *Nothing but the Truth*] who will work out (run) for a couple of hours. . . . Second, there is no way a sprinter will fun for six miles, especially in the rain. (*Negative*)

As discussed earlier, kinetic responses represent, according to Bogdan (1992), a partial response to the *form* of the literary work. The work is evaluated or judged favorably or unfavorably in terms of whether readers perceive the rhetorical strategies of the author as effective or not effective. Students may complain about formal deficiencies of the work, create parallels between the dialogue of the characters and how "real-life" people would talk at a certain age or in certain situations, anticipate the evolution of the plot, or stereotype characters according to ideology (e.g., "how typically female"). Patterns suggest that readers have already formulated how they connect with the text in terms of preconceived aesthetic criteria:

Immediately I knew this was a narrative account of events that had already transpired.

I had an idea . . . how the characters might respond given that time in history and the conventions that ruled the period.

Two of the three novels seem to have the same style of ending.

As with stock responses, one senses some resistance to the novels, but the kinetic responders hold off full engagement by evaluating the extent to which the work meets their own aesthetic requirements. Bogdan (1992) argues that such responses are always made relative to how familiar or unfamiliar the author's rhetorical structures and language are to students.

Critical Response

Stasis and partial responses are identified by Bogdan (1992) as "precritical responses" (p. 121). She defines the critical response as beginning where

"the precritical response leaves off when a class is ready to supplant ex-
changing initial responses to a story with a more precise *measuring* of their
responses against a closer look at the text" (p. 121; emphasis added). In
the ideal classroom, the "welter of real experience would be . . . transmuted
into literary experience as students take their foray into the literary world
with a view to differences from, rather than similarities with, the world of
ordinary life" (p. 121).

Critical responses may reveal a blend of stasis and critical appreciation that acknowledges the power of the text on the reader as well as an
understanding of *why* the text exercises that power. As the following responses indicate, we could perceive these readers as having been able to
enter the circle of the fictional world while retaining an awareness of the
role that the author's crafting has played in that entry:

> It must be unscrupulous of me, but that's the joy of reading a book;
> it is an escape from the world as we know it, one where anything is
> possible.

> Gary Paulsen uses the setting of the island . . . to teach Wil and the
> reader about harmony, serenity, and reality in life.

> This second time through, it was evident that Avi was setting us up.

> An important point . . . is the selection of facts has been very
> carefully made by the author.

> The author is consistent in her point of view . . . [which] helps to
> spell out the theme as we experience her life through her eyes.

These responses seem to suggest a "caring about the text" in a way
that illustrates how texts work on readers (Scholes, 1985, p. 149). The responses also indicate how far these readers have gone toward becoming
members of the literary reading community. They reflect the kind of pleasure in the workings of aesthetic effects that we also find in the experienced listener of hard rock, jazz, folk music, or opera. These readers appear to know *why* the work affects them the way it does. Judgments are
suspended to allow the work to exercise its effect, and even the unfamiliar can be entertained until the reader finds some way of connecting it to
the larger matrix of his or her reading experience. Readers who have
reached this end of the response continuum can be more patient and accepting and typically work *with* the text.

RESPONSE AND CRITICISM: AN INTERPLAY

Although stock and kinetic responses may reflect partial response by readers, I am not implying that these categories carry negative meaning. They are *descriptive* and, of course, *interpretive*, based on my own reading of my students' statements. My intent, as suggested earlier, was to find a way of understanding and interpreting the nature of my students' responses so that I could more appropriately respond to them as a teacher. However, in making an attempt to *locate* student responses on a continuum, we are restricted by that continuum and its boundaries. As such, it is not an entirely reliable indicator of where students are as readers of literature, if for no other reason than that the nature of their responses can differ widely when reading *other* literary texts. Hines's (1997) "multiplicity of response" (p. 131) is a concept that applies not only to the responses of a whole class of students but also to each individual student as he or she reads multiple texts.

However, might we also not resist the tendency to make linear and hierarchical what is often multilayered, equivocating, and "deeply felt," as Bogdan and colleagues (1997, p. 98) argue? When we make students' responses linear and hierarchical in the ways I have done in this chapter—however noble my intention—are we not in danger of suggesting that this is *all* they are capable of at any given stage? What happens, for example, when we consider a structuralist critique of *Death of a Salesman* using the foregoing categories? Formal criticism has always shrouded itself with an aura of authority, as if it is outside the limitations of "other" readers (that is, nonprofessional critics). Is it not possible, for instance, to suggest that the following example of a supposedly *pure* structural analysis of Arthur Miller's *Death of a Salesman* (1949) also contains evidence of reader-based assertions?

> Arthur Miller's *Death of a Salesman* concerns the Loman family. Willy is a failed businessman whose sons, Biff and Happy, are also failures largely through their father's bad influence. The play concludes with Willy's suicide. The Great American Dream is embodied in Willy's dead brother, Ben [sic] who went into the jungle at 18 and came out very rich at 21 and appears to Willy from time to time in the play. The Lomans' lack of business success is paralleled by moral failures. Biff's prospects are ruined early by petty thieving, which Willy makes light of, reassuring Biff that what matters is having the right image and being 'well thought of.' (Selden, 1989, p. 57)

The claims made (e.g., Willy is a failed businessman, the Lomans' lack of business success is paralleled by moral failures) appear to be textually based, but the significance of the parallel structures that are identified must be inferred. Even critics will attach different significances to textual elements. In that attachment lies a response. I do not see the following example from one of my students as being essentially different from the one above:

> The fact that Jane [Eyre] had no family and very few friends leads us to believe that she is searching for love and belonging in this world. So when we experience her relationship with Rochester and her coincidental meeting and discover of St. John, Diana, and Mary Rivers, the theme (of love and belonging) becomes well illustrated. It is then confirmed in the end when she is finally able to marry Rochester. She has found love and a place to belong.

Perhaps our task should be to help students know *how* we all come to these inferences and to understand how the interplay of the state of our knowledge at the time, our values, and our preferences as readers all have a role in how we infer what the text means to us. One way of doing this is through an assignment such as the one described in this chapter. By having the students "unpack" the differences between their responses and their seemingly objective critiques, they actually saw greater connections between the two than differences:

> I think a major strength of a reader-based perspective is that it really gets my mind working, thinking about the connections I made with the text and why I made these connections.

> I have found it nearly impossible to discuss literature without some aspect of the self entering into it. Responses my students make serve as springboards for analytical discussion, and sometimes analytic elements appear as part of a response. The blurring of the lines between the two perspectives seems to support my view that neither perspective is really exclusive of the other.

Furthermore, the students also exhibited a greater range of types of response than we might typically expect. That is, the opportunity to *articulate* their connections with the texts makes them conscious of the variety of ways in which we naturally approach them. This, in turn, enabled the students to better understand not only the potential role of personal response in the classroom but also the potential subjectivity of critique. The following statements came from the same student in the same paper on Sonia Levitin's *The Return* (1987):

As the Beta Yisrael refugees struggle to survive, they are, at crucial junctures in the novel, faced with the necessity of violating some of the most cherished rules of their faith.

As a reader, I almost wanted to scream out too (as Desta did when she and her aunt are insulted because they are Jewish), because even though Desta and her aunt may never have existed, I know that this conversation, or one like it, has taken place through time in countless languages and many different countries.

The power of cultural relativism is not merely that it helps understanding groups with other life-styles, but that it defines and strengthens one's self-concept by allowing the individual to position him/herself in relation to others. In *The Return*, Sonia Levitin has written a book that can help American students become more sensitive to their own position in relation to that of other peoples through the exploration of a culture that most of them will likely find alien.

I found the book to be very warm and authentic. Since it was based on a real situation, it was more meaningful than if it had been total fabrication. It made me, as a reader, more interested to know that people like Desta really exist and that many of them made the same journey as described in this story.

The first example could be categorized as critical response, focusing on the textual information in a seemingly objective way. The second example may be classified as stasis in that the distance between the reader and the text is merely a physical one—the reader is completely in the world of the text. In the third, we return to criticism as we would normally perceive it; and in the fourth, we find an example of a stock response wherein the reader relates elements of the text in a conscious way to what he knows about Operation Moses, the secret airlift of Ethiopian Jews to Israel in 1985. Such variety in response was typical of the many students who have completed this assignment.

CONCLUSION

In commencing the literary dialectic with the reader's response, we give our students the clearest indication that our classrooms are places in which they play a vital role in that dialectic. As I found with my students, when

I encouraged them to consider their responses *reflectively* I was creating an opportunity for them to consider their responses seriously, not just as a token opportunity for them to air their views. When we do this, we create a context in which reflective response naturally connects with critical response. When this happens we open the literary dialectic (Bogdan et al., 1997) to allow us to focus on what is involved in any act of reading literature—acts of engagement, the interplay of knowledge about what is read and aesthetic response, the interplay of knowledge about how we read and how we respond. In the latter half of Bogdan's (1992) work, we find her struggling with distinctions in the kinds of responses readers have, delineating differences (as I have done in this chapter) only to find that, despite our best intentions, these distinctions potentially *undermine* what the reader actually brings to and from the text. Bogdan and colleagues (1997) argue that rather than the alternation between engagement and detachment, which Bogdan (1992) struggled with in her earlier work, the literary dialectic

> requires teachers to be able to support each other's and students' learning through curious twists and turns, which include fragile, frightening awakenings and stubborn, indefatigable forgettings. (Bogdan et al., 1997, p. 91)

As we create bridges to help our students in that transmutation process, we also empower them to begin not only to understand the nature of literary criticism but also to see *their own role in interpretational play as vital in the development of their understanding and appreciation of literature.*

APPENDIX

Literary Texts Cited

Avi. (1990). *The true confessions of Charlotte Doyle.* New York: Avon.

Avi. (1991). *Nothing but the truth.* New York: Avon.

Brontë, C. (1960). *Jane Eyre.* New York: Penguin. (Original work published 1847)

Brontë, E. (1947). *Wuthering Heights.* New York: Bantam. (Original work published 1847)

Carter, F. (1985). *The education of Little Tree.* Albuquerque, NM: University of New Mexico Press.

Cleaver, V., & Cleaver, B. (1969). *Where the lilies bloom.* New York: HarperKeypoint.

Collier, J. L., & Collier, C. (1974). *My brother Sam is dead.* New York: Scholastic.

Cormier, R. (1974). *The chocolate war.* New York: Dell.

Cormier, R. (1977). *I am the cheese.* New York: Dell.

Cormier, R. (1983). *The bumblebee flies anyway.* New York: Dell.

Cormier, R. (1985). *Beyond the chocolate war.* New York: Dell.

Go, S. (1985). *Requiem* (G. Harcourt, Trans.). Tokyo and New York: Kodansha International.

Goethe, W. (1949). *The sorrows of young Werther* (V. Lange, Trans.). New York: Rinehart & Co. (Original work published 1774)

Hughes, R. (1929). *A high wind in Jamaica.* New York: Harper and Row.

Hunt, I. (1970). *No promises in the wind.* New York: Berkeley Books.

Knowles, J. (1968). *Phineas.* New York: Bantam.

Levitin, S. (1987). *The return.* New York: Fawcett Juniper.

Lowry, L. (1993). *The giver.* New York: Bantam.

Mazer, A. (1993). (Ed.). *America street: A multicultural anthology of stories.* New York: Persea Books.

Miller, A. (1949). *Death of a salesman.* New York: Penguin.

Myers, W. D. (1988). *Fallen angels.* New York: Scholastic.

Myers, W. D. (1992). *Somewhere in the darkness.* New York: Scholastic.

O'Brien, C. (1974). *Z for Zachariah.* New York: Macmillan.

Paterson, K. (1980). *Jacob have I loved.* New York: Avon.

Paterson, K. (1991). *Lyddie.* New York: Puffin.

Paulsen, G. (1988). *The island.* New York: Dell.

Rochman, H. (1988). *Somehow tenderness survives.* New York: HarperKeypoint.

Thomas, J. C. (1990). (Ed.). *A gathering of flowers.* New York: HarperKeypoint.

Voigt, C. (1981). *Homecoming.* New York: Fawcett Juniper.

Voigt, C. (1982). *Dicey's song.* New York: Fawcett Juniper.

Zindel, P. (1968). *The pigman.* New York: Bantam.

References

Abrams, M. H. (1953). *The mirror and the lamp: Romantic theory and the critical tradition*. London: Oxford University Press.

Abrams, M. H. (1989). *Doing things with texts: Essays in criticism and critical theory* (M. Fisher, Ed.). New York and London: Norton.

Althusser, L. (1976). *Essays on ideology*. London: Verso.

Beach, R. (1991). *A teacher's introduction to reader-response theories*. Urbana, IL: National Council of Teachers of English.

Beach, R. (1997). Students' resistance to engagement with multicultural literature. In T. Rogers & A. O. Soter (Eds.), *Reading across cultures: Teaching literature in a diverse society*. New York: Teachers College Press.

Birch, D. (1989). *Language, literature and critical practice*. New York: Routledge.

Bishop, R. S. (1991). *Presenting Walter Dean Myers*. Boston: Twayne.

Bleich, D. (1978). *Subjective criticism*. Baltimore: Johns Hopkins University Press.

Bogdan, D. (1992). *Re-educating the imagination: Toward a poetics, politics, and pedagogy of literary engagement*. Portsmouth, NH: Boynton/Cook Heinemann.

Bogdan, D., Dark, H. E., & Robertson, J. (1997). Sweet surrender and trespassing desires in reading: Jane Campion's *The Piano* and the struggle for responsible pedagogy. *Changing English, 4*(1), 81–103.

Booth, W. (1983). *The rhetoric of fiction* (2nd ed.). Chicago: University of Chicago Press.

Chodorow, N. (1978). *The reproduction of mothering*. Berkeley: University of California Press.

Crane, R. S. (1953). *The language of criticism and the structure of poetry*. Toronto: University of Toronto Press.

Cuddon, J. A. (1991). *A dictionary of literary terms*. Oxford: Cambridge University Press.

Culler, J. (1982). *On deconstruction: Theory and criticism after structuralism*. Ithaca, NY: Cornell University Press.

Dasenbrook, R. W. (1992). Teaching multicultural literature. In J. Trimmer & T. Warnock (Eds.), *Understanding others: Cultural and cross-cultural studies and the teaching of literature* (pp. 35–46). Urbana, IL: National Council of Teachers of English.

de Man, P. (1989). Semiology and rhetoric. In D. Richter (Ed.), *The critical tradition: Classic texts and contemporary trends* (pp. 1011–1021). New York: St. Martin's Press.

Derrida, J. (1982). *Margins of philosophy*. Chicago: University of Chicago Press.

Donelson, K. L., & Nilsen, A. P. (1995). *Literature for today's young adults* (5th ed.). Glenview, IL: Scott Forsman.

Eagleton, T. (1983). *Literary theory: An introduction*. Minneapolis: University of Minnesota Press.

Ellis, J. E. (1989). *Against deconstruction*. Princeton, NJ: Princeton University Press.

Erikson, E. (1963). *Childhood and society*. Princeton, NJ: Princeton University Press.

Fairbanks, C. M. (1995). Reading students: Texts in context. *English Education, 27*(1), 40–52.

Fetterley, J. (1978). *The resisting reader: A feminist approach to American fiction*. Bloomington: Indiana University Press.

Foreman, J., & Shumway, D. R. (1992). Cultural studies: Reading visual texts. In J. Berlin (Ed.), *Cultural studies in the English classroom* (pp. 244–261). Portsmouth, NH: Boynton/Cook Heinemann.

Foucault, M. (1988). What is an author? (J. P. Harari, Trans.). In D. Lodge (Ed.), *Modern criticism and theory* (pp. 196–210). New York: Longman. (Original work published in 1979)

Fowler, R. (1977). *Linguistics and the novel*. London: Methuen.

Frye, N. (1954). *The anatomy of criticism*. Princeton, NJ: Princeton University Press.

Garratt, A., & McCue, H. (Eds.). (1989). *Authors and artists for young adults* (Vols. 1 and 2). Detroit: Gale Research.

Gibson, W. (1990). Contrarities of emotion, or five days with "Pride and Prejudice." In C. Moran & E. F. Penfield (Eds.), *Conversations: Contemporary critical theory and the teaching of literature* (pp. 114–119). Urbana, IL: National Council of Teachers of English.

Gilbert, S., & Gubar, S. (1979). *The madwoman in the attic: The woman writer and the nineteenth century literary imagination*. New Haven, CT: Yale University Press.

Gilligan, C. (1982). *In a different voice: Psychological theory and women's development*. Cambridge, MA: Harvard University Press.

Godzich, W. (1994). *The culture of literacy*. Cambridge, MA: Harvard University Press.

Green, K., & LeBihan, J. (1996). *Critical theory and practice: A coursebook*. London and New York: Routledge.

Greenblatt, S. (1980). *Renaissance self-fashioning*. Chicago: University of Chicago Press.

Grossman, P. (1990). *The making of a teacher: Teacher knowledge and teacher education*. New York: Teachers College Press.

Hawkes, T. (1977). *Structuralism and semiotics*. Berkeley and Los Angeles: University of California Press.

Hines, M. B. (1997). Multiplicity and difference in literary inquiry: Toward a conceptual framework for reader-centered cultural criticism. In T. Rogers & A. O. Soter (Eds.), *Reading across cultures: Teaching literature in a diverse society* (pp. 116–134). New York: Teachers College Press.

Holland, N. (1975). *5 readers reading*. New Haven, CT: Yale University Press.

Holland, N. (1980). Unity, identity, text, self. In J. Tompkins (Ed.), *Reader response criticism* (pp. 118–133). Baltimore: Johns Hopkins University Press.

Hynds, S. (1990). Reading as a social event: Comprehension and response in the text, classroom, and world. In D. Bogdan & S. B. Straw (Eds.), *Beyond com-*

munication: Reading comprehension and criticism (pp. 237–256). Portsmouth, NH: Boynton/Cook.

Iser, W. (1989). *Prospecting: From reader response to literary anthropology.* Baltimore: Johns Hopkins University Press.

Jauss, H. H. (1982). *Aesthetic experience and literary hermeneutics.* Minneapolis, MN: University of Minnesota Press.

Kaplan, E. A. (1988). (Ed.). *Postmodernism and its discontents.* London and New York: Verso.

Kolodny, A. (1985). Dancing through the minefield. In E. Showalter (Ed.), *The new feminist criticism: Essays on women, literature and theory* (pp. 361–377). London: Routledge.

Kundera, M. (1988). *The art of the novel.* New York: Harper & Row.

Lacan, J. (1988). The insistence of the letter in the subconscious. In D. Lodge (Ed.), *Modern criticism and theory* (pp. 79–106). New York: Longman. (Original work published 1966)

Leitch, V. B. (1992). *Cultural criticism, literary theory, poststructuralism.* New York: Columbia University Press.

Lodge, D. (1988). (Ed.). *Modern criticism and theory.* New York: Longman.

Lynn, S. (1990). "A passage into critical theory." In C. Moran & E. F. Penfield (Eds.), *Conversations: Contemporary critical theory and the teaching of literature* (pp. 99–113). Urbana, IL: National Council of Teachers of English.

Miller, N. (1986). *Subject to change: Reading feminist writing.* New York: Columbia University Press.

Mitchell, J. (1988). Feminity, narrative as psychoanalysis. In D. Lodge (Ed.), *Modern criticism and theory* (pp. 425–431). New York: Longman.

Monseau, V., & Salvner, G. M. (1992). *Reading their world: The young adult novel in the classroom.* Portsmouth, NH: Boynton/Cook Heinemann.

Montrose, L. (1992). New historicisms. In S. Greenblatt & G. Gunn (Eds.), *Redrawing the boundaries: The transformation of English and American literary studies* (pp. 392–418). New York: Modern Language Association.

Pearson, C. (1989). *The hero within: Six archetypes we live by* (2nd ed.). San Francisco: HarperSanFrancisco.

Phelan, J. (1994). A conversation. *Ohio Journal of English Language Arts, 35*(2), 37–42.

Phelan, J. (1996). *Narrative as rhetoric: Technique, audiences, ethics, ideology.* Columbus, OH: The Ohio State University Press.

Probst, R. (1990). *Response and analysis: Teaching literature in junior and senior high school* (2nd ed.). Portsmouth, NH: Boynton/Cook Heinemann.

Purves, A. C., Rogers, T., & Soter, A. O. (1995). *How porcupines make love III: Readers, texts, cultures in the response-based literature classroom* (3rd ed.). New York: Longman.

Rabinowitz, P. (1976). Truth in fiction: A re-examination of audiences. *Critical Inquiry, 4,* 121–141.

Rabinowitz, P. (1987). *Before reading: Narrative conventions and the politics of interpretation.* Ithaca, NY: Cornell University Press.

Radford, J. (1992). Coming to terms: Dorothy Richardson, modernism and women. In P. Brooker (Ed.), *Modernism/postmodernism* (pp. 95–106). New York: Longman.

Rich, A. (1972). When we dead awaken: Writing as re-vision. *College English, 34*(18), 18–30.

Richards, I. A. (1929). *Practical criticism.* New York: Harcourt Brace Jovanovich.

Richter, D. H. (1989). *The critical tradition: Classic texts and contemporary trends.* New York: St. Martin's Press.

Rogers, T. (1997). No imagined peaceful place: A story of community, texts, and cultural conversations in one urban high school English classroom. In T. Rogers & A. Soter (Eds.), *Reading across cultures: Teaching literature in a diverse society* (pp. 95–115). New York: Teachers College Press.

Rogers, T., & Soter, A. O. (1997). (Eds.). (1997). *Reading across cultures: Teaching literature in a diverse society* (pp. 1–9). New York: Teachers College Press.

Rogers, T., & Soter, A. O. (1998, August). *Reading across cultures: Teaching literature in a diverse society.* Paper delivered at the Third International Conference for Global Conversations on Language and Literature, Bordeaux, France.

Rosenblatt, L. M. (1978). *The reader, the text, the poem: The transactional theory of the literary work.* Carbondale: Southern Illinois University Press.

Sarup, M. (1992). *Jacques Lacan.* Toronto: University of Toronto Press.

Scholes, R. (1985). *Textual power: Literary theory and the teaching of English.* New Haven, CT, and London: Yale University Press.

Scholes, R. (1989). *Protocols of reading.* New Haven, CT, and London: Yale University Press.

Schumacher, D. (1989). Subjectivities: A theory of the critical process. In J. Donovan (Ed.), *Feminist literary criticism: Explorations in theory* (2nd ed.; pp. 29–37). Lexington: University of Kentucky Press.

Selden, R. (1989). *Practicing theory and reading literature: An introduction.* Lexington: University of Kentucky Press.

Selden, R., & Widdowson, P. (1993). *A reader's guide to contemporary literary theory.* Lexington: University of Kentucky Press.

Shlovsky, V. (1990). *Theory of prose* (B. Sher, Trans.). Elmwood, IL: Dalkey Archive Press.

Showalter, E. (1977). *A literature of their own: British women novelists from Bronte to Lessing.* Princeton, NJ: Princeton University Press.

Showalter, E. (1985). *The new feminist criticism: Essays on women, literature and theory.* New York: Pantheon.

Soter, A. O. (1996). Applying critical perspectives to *My Brother Sam Is Dead* and *Where the Lilies Bloom. Focus, 22,* 59–66.

Soter, A. O. (1997). Reading literature of other cultures: Some issues in critical interpretation. In T. Rogers & A. O. Soter (Eds.), *Reading across cultures: Teaching literature in a diverse society* (pp. 213–230). New York: Teachers College Press.

Soter, A. O., & Letcher, M. (1998). Literary theory and appreciation: Learning about the literary craft. *Journal of Children's Literature, 24*(2), 22–31.

Stevens, B. K., & Stewart, L. (1992). *A guide to literary criticism and research* (2nd ed.). New York: Holt, Rinehart & Winston.

Stimpson, C. (1992). Feminist criticism. In S. Greenblatt & J. Gunn (Eds.), *Redrawing the boundaries: The transformation of English and American studies* (pp. 251–269). New York: Modern Language Association.

Strickland, G. (1981). *Structuralism or criticism: Thoughts on how we read.* London: Cambridge University Press.

Tompkins, J. P. (1980). *Reader-response criticism: From formalism to post-structuralism.* Baltimore: Johns Hopkins University Press.

Torsney, C. B. (1989). The critical quilt: Alternative authority in feminist criticism. In G. D. Atkins & L. Morrow (Eds.), *Contemporary literary theory* (pp. 180–199). Amherst: University of Massachusetts Press.

Trimmer, J., & Warnock, T. (Eds.). (1992). *Understanding others: Cultural and cross-cultural studies and the teaching of literature.* Urbana, IL: National Council of Teachers of English.

Wimsatt, W. K., & Beardsely, M. C. (1954). *The verbal icon: Studies in the meaning of poetry.* Lexington: University of Kentucky Press.

Wolf, M. (1992). *A thrice-told tale: Feminism, postmodernism and ethnographic responsibility.* Stanford, CA: Stanford University Press.

Index

About the Author

Anna Soter is Associate Professor in Language, Literacy and Culture and English Education at The Ohio State University. Her specializations include literary theory in schools, young adult literature, comparative discourse, teacher learning, and the teaching of literature and writing. She previously taught English in Australian secondary schools, and among courses she currently teaches are children's and young adult literature, the teaching of literature and writing in secondary schools, and cultural aspects of literacy learning. She is co-editor with Theresa Rogers of *Reading Across Cultures* (1997) and co-author with Alan C. Purves and Theresa Rogers of *How Porcupines Make Love III* (1990, 1995). Other publications include articles and chapters in various journals and edited collections.